MAKING IT TO THE

Altar

MAKING IT TO THE

Altar

From Cyber To Ceremony

Our Story: Our Love. Our Life.
Our Lessons.

Richard E. & Nicole Y. Lawrence

R&N Publishing

R&N Publishing   Columbus, Ohio

Richard E. & Nicole Y. Lawrence/R&N Publishing
Columbus, Ohio/43232
www.foreveryoungblackandmarried.com

Publisher's Note: Although every precaution has been taken to verify the accuracy of the information contained herein, the author and publisher assume no responsibility for any errors or omissions. No liability is assumed for damages that may result from the use of information contained within.

Information and materials available in this publication are for informational use only. The information entailed is designed to provide accurate and authoritative information with regard to the subject matter covered. It is provided with the understanding that the publisher is not engaged in rendering legal, accounting, or other professional advice. If legal advice or other expert assistance is required, the services of a competent professional person should be sought.
-From a *Declaration of Principles*
jointly adopted by a Committee of the American Bar Association and a Committee of Publishers and Associations

Books may be purchased by contacting the publisher and author at:
www.foreveryoungblackandmarried.com

Cover Design: Nicole Y. Lawrence.
Photographer: Candis Absalon
Publisher: R&N Publishing a division of Forever Young, Black & Married LLC., Columbus, Ohio
Editor: Richard E. & Nicole Y. Lawrence
ISBN: 978-0-9969067-0-8(Paperback)
ISBN: 978-0-9969067-1-5(Ebook)
ISBN:978-0-9969067-2-2(Hardback)
First Edition printed: 2015
Printed in United States of America
Making It To The Altar: From Cyber To Ceremony Our Story: Our Love. Our Life. Our Lessons./ Richard E. & Nicole Y. Lawrence.-- 1st ed.

We would like to dedicate *"Making It To The Altar"* to all our friends and family that genuinely supported us over the years, you have truly been a blessing to both our lives and our marriage. To all the supportive family of Young, Black and Married the online community; none of this would be possible without you. Thank you for recognizing the value in our message and sharing your testimonies with us. Many of you all say we're a blessing to your life but the truth is we're the blessed ones!

"You come to love not by finding the perfect person, but by seeing an imperfect person perfectly."
~Sam Keen

CONTENTS

PROLOGUE

Everyone wants and deserves to be loved, not everyone knows how to love. At twenty-three years old I had to be honest with myself I had absolutely no idea how to properly give or receive love. I was a mess and what made it worse was that I had no one to blame but myself. I was hurting people with my "love," because I never recovered from the moment someone hurt me with theirs.

I was out partying the night I met the woman who'd become my wife in a nightclub in the summer of 2005. Nicole Singleton. I thought she was beautiful but I was attracted to the way she carried herself. I felt something in that moment. We talked and laughed at the bar while I waited for my drink. We exchanged names, not numbers. When the bar-tender returned with my drink I nodded my head and politely said goodnight because I never thought I'd see her again. I thought to myself, "She's nice," and that was that. Then one lonely night in April of 2006 I was in a chat room looking for someone to talk to and soon after logging in I got a private message from, 'Pretty Thickness.' "Remember me?" It was the girl I'd met in Ohio at the bar.

Nicole and I became friends in a chat room, fell in love through phone calls and developed an unbreakable friendship. Two years and 400 miles would stand between the initial meeting and the next time we'd laid eyes on each other. On the 10th day we physically spent together I proposed. During a year-long engagement stones would be cast, mountains would be moved and failure would become awkwardly familiar but we made it over that broom. Funny thing about life is that it is an excellent teacher. I pray that the lessons life has shared with Nicole and I can help someone else along their way.

This is our story: Our love. Our life. Our lessons.

CHAPTER ONE

Finding Friendship

Nicole and I are best-friends! I've found over the years that for us it has been our friendship and not our love that has sustained our bond. Before we were married it was our friendship that reunited us after an eleven month break up. I remember coming back into Nicole's life with no expectation only hopes of being friends. In the months Nicole and I weren't speaking I felt like my confidant was missing. For a while I thought it'd be possible to replace her but I was wrong. Nicole and I are best friends and our relationship has taught me that a healthy friendship is an integral part of a lasting marriage. Let's review. Nicole and I first met in the summer of 2005. I made a road trip with an old friend of mine leaving Rochester, NY headed to Dayton, Ohio. It was a weekend trip nothing major just leaving town to party with some people my friend knew. While attending that party I first met Nicole. At the time Nicole was in her junior year at Central State University, which was fifteen to twenty minutes away from Dayton.

Our first meeting didn't mean much to me at the time, but over the years I'd learn that it was just the first observation of many things that makes Nicole special to me. I met her at the bar as I was waiting for the bartender to serve me. She could see that I was becoming frustrated but I wasn't the type to speak up so she asked me what I was drinking, took my money and ordered for me. When the bartender returned, she handed me my drink and change and we laughed for a few seconds. I told her my name, she told me hers. I asked her if she had a boyfriend and she told me she did. We talked a little while longer and politely went our separate ways. I can honestly say that I never expected to see, "the chick from Central State" again. I probably wouldn't have but Nicole and I both had something in common; we were internet addicts. She enjoyed playing online games; I enjoyed chat rooms (the precursor to social media lol.)

It was in a chat room that Nicole and I would randomly meet again. One evening I was chatting when I received a private message from, 'PrettyThickness' Nicole's online name at the time. Her first words were simply, "Remember me?" I honestly don't remember the conversation we had that night, I just remember that it was refreshing. Neither of us hit on each other we just talked about our goals and plans for life. I asked her major in college and she told me Electronic Media/Communications. I've always loved to write so I was interested. I could tell from reading her thoughts that Nicole was not only a writer but an excellent one. That was my initial attraction which sounds weird because I've always found my wife gorgeous but it was her mind that drew me in. To be honest I genuinely thought she'd never be interested in me. I told myself, "She's too pretty, she'd never want you." I guess that made it easier to accept the thought of rejection but I found myself talking to this young lady well into the morning. She ended our conversation by telling me she was going to sleep to prepare for class later that morning so we said our goodbyes. Much like our initial in person meeting our first online meeting ended with no guarantee of ever interacting again. Although this time we had talked longer and started the process of getting to know each other, Nicole was still in a relationship and I had just gotten over a bad breakup so our conversation was purely friendly. I assumed I was being placed in the "friend-zone" anyway.

In those first few months of really getting to know one another it seemed like Nicole and I discussed everything. Sometimes I think the distance was helpful you know? It felt like I was talking to someone who couldn't judge me because they didn't really know me. I would later come to understand that just because Nicole and I hadn't spent time together physically didn't mean she didn't know me better than anyone in this world. These days I look back and realize my wife knows me so well because she had the ability to get me to open up. I had never truly opened up to anyone before. Openness and vulnerability are the true meaning of intimacy, not sexual intercourse as I had led myself to believe prior to meeting my wife. Meeting Nicole made me realize just how much of a mess I was. The crazy thing is at that time you couldn't tell me I didn't have my life together. I truly believed I was accomplishing something substantial. I was leaving home everyday to head to a job that was tolerable but not exciting. I enjoyed the job but I was far from passionate about it. I was attending graduate classes to major in a field I never wanted a career in while running around from woman to woman looking for the sort of love I was incapable of giving. I didn't love myself and couldn't admit I was unhappy. If there is one thing marriage has taught me it's that you cannot love someone the way they require if you don't love yourself first.

When I met Nicole I was unstable. I was incapable of loving myself because my entire self worth was wrapped up in the women I was sleeping with, the car I drove, the clothes I wore, how much money I had and how educated I was. My entire being was based on superficial things which in the end caused me more pain than happiness. I don't know when I became aware of my flaws but what I do know is that it didn't take Nicole long to see through the fake display of self confidence I put on in an attempt to attract her. She used to ask me all the time in those early stages of friendship, "Richard, who are you?" The truth was that when Nicole and I met I was twenty-three years old and fresh out of a four-year relationship that had really taken a toll on me emotionally. I had no idea who I was and honestly I had no business dating but I continued to do so in an attempt to fill the loneliness I felt. It didn't work but that never stopped me from trying. Through those early days of conversation with Nicole the thing I tried hardest to do was hide my true self. The Richard I was ashamed of. Nicole saw through the façade or the representative as many folks call it. My representative didn't impress her because she sought to explore the person I really was. Her willingness to get to know me, more importantly to love the person she got to know has been the biggest blessing in my life. If there's one thing I'm sure of it's that I am not an easy person to love.

I believe too many couples don't take the adequate time to properly get to know each other, myself included for the majority of my dating years. Often I'd go on a dinner date or out to the movies where no real conversation takes place or we'd just sit at one another's house and watch movies; Netflix and Chill but before Netflix so I guess DVD and chill? Nicole always calls it "college" dating. A lot of times when you're in college you sit around in your dorm broke hoping your boyfriend/girlfriend comes over. Movies, dinner, hanging out and sex is about all those relationships equate to. Many adult relationships these days aren't much different from the "kid" version. I think a lot of people become infatuated with people they don't really know just because they've spent a lot of time together, or they're so desperately wanting love. They may have spent time together but it was always fun time, time with no actual substance. The long-distance friendship Nicole and I were beginning to form left us in a spot where we had nothing but "get to know you" time because we couldn't see each other. Neither of us was really in a position financially to visit. Nicole had a boyfriend when we first met and I was involved with a young lady on my end however, no matter how much time I spent with the lady I was seeing, I was talking to Nicole more. Until I finally realized that I actually knew more about Nicole than I knew about the young lady I had spent the last three years, off-and-on having fun with.

Nicole and I were talking more as friends than I was talking to my girlfriend. Eventually Nicole and I both would end our relationships, but not for each other. We realized we were using our then significant others as space fillers. Our friendship was at an impasse because I didn't want it to progress further than friendship and I was starting to believe Nicole wanted more. I started getting scared of what I felt was going to come; pressure to date. Looking back I realize that my fear was unwarranted. Had I trusted my wife with my intentions perhaps our relationship would have taken a different course in those earlier stages yet through it all we were progressing. Nicole was truly becoming my best-friend. I'd call her at least four to five times a week and we'd talk about everything from work to politics, religion, movies, music, poetry, fashion, sports but most importantly we talked about family. Nicole and I would sit for hours and talk about our families. It was in November of 2006 Nicole told me that she loved me. She told me I didn't have to tell her that I loved her too she just wanted me to know that she loved and cared about me. I always took it to mean she was "in love" with me and wanted a relationship when what Nicole really meant was that she valued our friendship. I didn't understand that at the time. I was so used to women wanting a relationship that I didn't realize I had a genuine friend who was concerned about me. I think that was the first occurrence of miscommunication in our relationship. Instead of asking Nicole for clarity on what she meant I assumed I knew. It wouldn't be until years later after we were married that I would ask. However, to Nicole's benefit she knew I was hesitant and she never pressured me into a relationship. She always left the decision up to me whether or not we'd move further. She never stopped going out on dates or put her life on hold waiting around for me and I found that attractive. We were having these deep conversations getting to know one another intimately but Nicole was not "stuck" on me. If I didn't ask her to be my girlfriend it was becoming clear she wasn't going to make the first move.

Although I never asked Nicole out I did ask her a lot of other important questions and she did the same with me. I remember Nicole asking me, "What do you want to do with your life?" I feel that's a very important question for a woman to ask a man who she's interested in early on in their courtship. I told Nicole I wanted to be general manager of the Chicago Bulls. I had never told any woman that before because I always figured they'd just laugh at me. Nicole didn't laugh she just asked, "How to you plan on achieving that?" I believe my answer began to let Nicole know who I was. I told Nicole that I had recently been accepted into graduate school majoring in Inclusive Childhood education grades 1-6 and I was going to be a teacher, then after I got my degree in teaching my plan was to become certified as an administrator and become an athletic director at the high school level and see what happened from there. That answer led to Nicole's next question, "Do you think that's the best route to achieving your dream?" I'll never forget that question or the conversation because I believe that night was the moment I fell in love with my wife. I felt like she was interested in me and never in my life had I felt like a woman was truly interested in me and that was all I ever wanted.

I sat and thought on her question. I really had to ask myself, were the things I was doing the best path towards my goal? I had to be truthful, none of the things I was doing were going to get me to my goals. My parents and other people around me told me that I would make a good teacher and I allowed them to sway me into a career I never wanted. I don't blame anyone I've come to realize all they wanted was what they thought would be best for me. I was working as a Teacher's Assistant at the time and people thought I was good at my job. They were encouraging me to pursue a teaching career because it seemed to be a good fit but that was never what I wanted and I would later come to find that doing things I didn't want to do only leaves me unhappy and resentful. Nicole's questions brought about self evaluation for me. Our friendship was of great benefit to me as a person but more importantly our friendship was the building block for our marriage. As unconventional as it may have been, our friendship helped us to know one another on a deeper level than we'd ever known anyone else.

If you're really interested in a person, I believe there are certain questions you should ask! I know it sounds ridiculous, but I believe there are at minimum fifteen questions you should be asking the person you're seriously dating. The questions don't have to be asked all in one conversation. In the case of Nicole and I we asked questions over a prolonged period of phone conversations. Those were our "dates" but I believe that regardless of where or how you meet someone, you have to ask questions to see if you're compatible with each other in enough of the important areas. I tell people all the time that equally yoked is not only a religious concept. I think people need to be equally yoked in their aspirations, beliefs and goals, that's the best way to find out if you've met your match. To close this chapter we've provided a list of fifteen questions we believe couples should ask each other while they're dating that can help assess whether or not they're on the same page. These questions are a great way for dating couples to take stock and see if marriage is on the horizon as well as providing a way for married couples to reconnect. If nothing else, they're great conversation topics.

* * *

Asking The Tough Questions *(Nicole)*

I am certain that afterwards many of you will think a number of the questions Richard and I asked each other are odd or maybe even irrelevant; well at some point and time we did too. We eventually realized that as much as we are alike we did not always share the same opinion. By asking even the simplest of questions it gave us a greater understanding of one another's priorities, preferences and logic. In a relationship disagreements are inevitable however, they are absolutely manageable! More importantly every disagreement does not have to end in an argument. One thing that I have found in the course of our marriage is that in the early stages we would fight and bicker regularly. After close observation I came to the realization that we habitually had the same argument under different pretences. It became crystal clear that no matter where the disagreement started it would ALWAYS end in the same fashion, surrounding the same topic(s). We decided that we needed to address and resolve the underlining issues head-on or else the constant squabbling would be the demise of our marriage and more importantly our friendship.

Revisiting the following list of questions allowed us to tap back into our similarities but more importantly discover, acknowledge and accept our differences, which then forced us to come to some type of suitable resolve versus ignoring the issue. When it all comes down to it, we had to do our work and any relationship that has a goal of happiness and longevity has to do their work as well. Doing the work is not an overnight process and by no means is it easy but it is in fact necessary. The goal of answering these questions is not to see how alike the two of you are, it is to stir up constructive conversation that hopefully leads to some very critical consciousness about yourself as well as your partner. These questions alone cannot determine whether the two of you are compatible but they can cause you to reflect deeply on the state of your relationship and whether or not it seems to be progressing or regressing.

15 Things You Should Discuss Before Getting Married

Our suggestion: each individual in addition to the provided questions, should create their own list with questions that are of great importance to them and make a copy to answer along with their partner. Next, sit down answer and discuss these questions including your own questions openly and honestly, with dialog and clarity being your sole objective. Be sure to document both sets of questions and answers. Store them in a secure place to revisit, re-read and even re-answer if necessary throughout your relationship. Always remember that who you are today is not who you'll be tomorrow if you live a life of evolution and maturation and the same goes for your partner. Keeping this notion at the forefront of your mind allows you to stay understanding of the person you fell in love with, while respecting and appreciating the person they're becoming. We have formatted the questions to be answered in an open dialogue between you and your partner.

1.) Are there any decisions in life you've made that you regret?
    If so, what have those experiences taught you?

2.) What has been your biggest weakness in past relationships?

3.) What has been your biggest hurdle in past relationships? How have you worked on that issue?

4.) Do you feel you can communicate with me about anything and without judgment?

5.) Do you think we're a good couple? Where do you see us five years from now?

6.) If we were experiencing problems in our relationship, would you be willing to seek counseling?

7.) How do you feel about gender roles? Are there responsibilities in a relationship you feel should be a "man's job" or a "woman's job?"

8.) What do you envision married life being? Do you still plan to hang out with friends, extended family and/or hobbies like you do now? Do you expect to spend most of your free time at home engaged with our family? Or some combination of the two?

9.) How do we handle money? Will we have joint accounts? Separate accounts? Some combination of both? How will we figure out savings, retirement, investments?

10.) In a marriage, what are your deal breakers? What situations would be an, "automatic" reason to divorce for you?

11.) How important is it to you that we are on good terms with each others' families?

12.) Do you have a close relationship with your family? Is there anyone in your family you have poor relations with/are estranged from?

13.) What are your career goals?

14.) Does your family have an influence over your relationship decisions? If so, how much?

15.) What relationship have you witnessed that you feel has impacted your views on relationships most? Was that impact a positive or negative one?

CHAPTER TWO

Communicate...Regardless!

Nicole and I asked each other questions and grew very close over the course of about six months. We were progressing as friends and possibly on our way to being a couple, at least that's what I told myself. I thought our relationship was fine just the way it was. Nicole loved me and I loved her. I figured she knew that I wanted to finish school, get myself together, have her come to New York to live with me and then we could start our life together. I had it all planned out in my mind however, what I would come to realize is that the dream I had planned out didn't align with reality. "They" say hindsight is 20/20 and as I get older I begin to truly understand what "they" mean. I had this perfect dream in my head but in reality I was avoiding a relationship with Nicole because commitment meant fidelity which was a concept I was foreign to. I had never been faithful to any woman and I honestly wanted to be different with Nicole but the distance separating us made it hard for me. Instead of telling Nicole how I was feeling I clung to a fantasy that sounded good because I thought it was what she wanted to hear. I was telling myself a lie that made it easiest to live in a manner I knew was wrong. I was willing to string along the heart of a woman I loved for fear of growing up. Nicole wasn't typical, she's never been typical. She never placed her life on hold waiting around for me to ask her to be my girlfriend. She was in school, pursuing a career in the music industry at that time, working and living her own life while looking forward to her college graduation. My wife didn't pursue me, she never felt as though it was her job to pursue me. If I wanted to be with her, I'd have to commit.

Nicole never told me that, she felt as though I should have known better. She felt that it should have been apparent to me if a relationship with her was what I wanted I needed to initiate it. Since Nicole wasn't the first one to say she wanted us to be together I allowed myself to believe she wasn't interested. As I said before, hindsight is 20/20 and looking back I see I was just making excuses because I was thinking with the wrong head. At that point in our relationship we were phone friends; pen pals with strong feelings who'd only met in person once. I didn't believe what Nicole and I had was, real, it felt too "right" almost reminiscent of a fairytale. I told myself maybe this was all just some childish puppy love that would pass with time. So I started moving away from her. I began calling less and tried to stop caring so much about someone I never spent any time with. Then life intervened. I received a phone call one night; Nicole had just been physically assaulted. I went from friend to grief counselor that evening. Her and I talked, cried and prayed into the wee-hours of the morning. I told her if there was anything she needed from me, anything that I could do for her, I would do it. I felt helpless and scared for my friend. She knew her attacker, he wasn't a stranger, she knew she would see this man again. That night all I could do was comfort.

Nicole. She wasn't the first person to disclose rape to me but she was the first person I loved to do so and that was horrifically different. I found myself feeling guilty about what had just happened to the woman I love. Feeling like, "If only I had been there to protect her..." I never shared those feelings of guilt with Nicole. Looking back I believe I held them to myself because I knew where the guilt really stemmed from. I don't know if I could have been there that night. I don't know if anything would have happened differently if I had committed to Nicole and relocated to Ohio for our relationship. What I do know is that on the night my friend came to me and shared the horror of what happened to her just an hour or so before the call; I was laid up with another woman. Nicole wasn't my girlfriend, she and I we weren't in a relationship. I had freedom to do what I thought would make me happy and then she was assaulted and I never felt more sad. I felt guilty. A man is supposed to provide and protect right? I was incapable of doing either and I felt Nicole was suffering via my faults. The selfish thoughts of a twenty-three year old boy who made the pain the woman he loved was going through all about him. She deserved better.

Instead of telling Nicole how I was feeling I kept it all inside. I thought she needed me to be strong in order to help her move past what she'd just been through. We continued talking every day after she was attacked. Eventually we talked past the event and tried to put it out of both our minds. I've learned now that even though we may have been talking daily we had stopped communicating openly. I had begun to close myself off in an attempt to deal with the way I was feeling because I didn't want to burden Nicole with my emotions; my feelings of uncertainty and guilt. Those feelings would come pouring out of me a few months later and not in a healthy way. I don't know who said it first; I just know it's true. Hearts are often broken by words left unspoken. January of 2007. I can't remember the day because it's a day I tried for years to forget. I look back and ask myself why and how I let our relationship fall apart over my lack of self control, compassion and love for the woman who truly meant the world to me? She was my best-friend and at times it felt like she was my only real friend and when my world needed me most. When she would reach out to me a second time to tell me she'd just been sexually assaulted by the same man and was locked in a bathroom hiding from her rapist. Instead of being there for her, instead of hopping in my car or on a plane to sit next to her and just hold her hand while she cried. What did I do? I blamed her for what had just happened.

I blamed my wife for another person's repulsiveness. I told her she shouldn't have been there, told her she should have called me as soon as the man showed up, not after he assaulted her. Told her she should have left the minute he walked in as if that would have mattered. What I should have been telling her was "I'm here for you!" I made her pain all about me because from the moment Nicole was attacked the first time I felt responsible. A part of me felt as though it was my duty to protect her because she was always looking out for me even when I didn't deserve her love and support. Nicole reached out for her friend to just listen; for her best-friend to be there when she needed a friend most and I failed her. I've been married to Nicole six years and I love that woman more than words could ever express. I am more hurt that I failed my friend at that moment in her life than at any other time including during our marriage. The friendship my wife and I share has always been the foundation of our love and I shattered that friendship because I didn't have the strength to think before I spoke or the wisdom to do what I should have done after being so mean; apologize. I did neither. What would occur next would be the most remarkable act of forgiveness that I ever experienced. Nicole called me a few days after her verbal assault. I cursed her out for what she'd been through as if she'd done something wrong and Nicole called me when I should have been the one calling her. I remember being home looking at the caller ID and I just deleted the call record. She left no voicemail. A short time later I would login to my MySpace page and there was a message from her in my inbox. I sat and stared at it for hours the first night I saw it and told myself there was no point in reading it because I knew she must be upset. I knew I was wrong but I didn't have the courage to be man enough to apologize. I cut off communication with my best-friend because of my mistakes and selfishness. With every day that went by after that conversation I felt like shit. Depression became real. Karma you know? At this point in our relationship I had only met Nicole once, got acquainted with her online in a chat room and spoken to her on the phone for about six or seven months; our relationship wasn't "real." That's the lie I believed in order to sleep at night.

Days passed until days turned to weeks and weeks into months. I never read Nicole's email but I went looking to see if she ever sent new ones; how arrogant of me. How arrogant to think that the woman I left would come back to me as if I were some sort of prize. I turned twenty-four in March of 2007 and I was still telling myself that any woman was lucky to have me. I used to say to myself, "I'm educated, I have a job, I'm in graduate school, I have no children; and I'm a twenty-four year old black man, I'm a woman's dream. It'd be easy to replace Nicole if she doesn't want me. I can find somebody just like her or better." Time would pass and prove me wrong. In those months without Nicole's friendship my life continued to spiral out of control. I couldn't find anyone close to meaning to me what Nicole meant to me. I just spent my time with anybody to say I had somebody. I hopped from woman to woman looking for love in the form of lust; self destructing and selfishly taking anyone who was unfortunate enough to cross my path along. I gradually stopped going to school until eventually I wasn't going at all. I was smoking weed excessively, drinking too much liquor and sleeping with women I barely knew. I honestly don't know what was going on with me back then but I know that as time went on I thought more and more about Nicole. I felt crazy thinking about her. I felt rejected, which is strange because I'm the one who rejected Nicole's earlier attempts to reach out to me. I had shut down and shut off. I believe that when people are hurting they try and disassociate from the pain thinking that avoidance will make it go away. That's what I was doing unsuccessfully. It took about eleven months for me to realize that I was the one who screwed up, and if I wanted a future with Nicole I had to be the one to make things right. I was scared of what she'd say to me. I told myself she had moved on and even if she did want me I didn't have anything to offer her. I was twenty-four years old, making $8.75 hourly, living with my parents and starting to flunk out of graduate school. I was feeling like a failure and then I got arrested for driving on a suspended license which only made me feel worse. As I sat in jail awaiting bail I began to think about Nicole. I remember telling her about some of the stupid things I'd done before we met and how she'd always say, "I wouldn't have let you do that." I know I was supposed to be able to discern right from wrong on my own, and I knew the things I was doing were wrong but I ignored my better judgment. I don't know if it was depression or if it was the guilt I was feeling about the things I had said to Nicole in January but I felt like I had nothing to live for.

I realized something about myself that night while sitting in a cell waiting to be bailed out. That night was when it hit me. The only person I felt comfortable talking to about anything authentic was Nicole. I got out of jail early the next morning and told myself I had to apologize to the woman I loved. It had been months since we'd last spoken. I logged into MySpace and checked my inbox, and there it was. That message from Nicole dated January 2007 that she had sent to me eleven months earlier. I finally mustered up the courage to read it. I just knew she was cursing me out for the things I said to her that night. I opened that message and it was very brief. It simply read, "Richard, I understand that news must have hurt you, I was hurt and I was scared. I felt like I could tell you. I'm not mad at you, I think we need to talk but if I never hear from you again, take care. I love you." I read that message a million times and every time I read it I felt like a fool. I went to bed that night and I prayed to God that if he showed me who I was supposed to be with; if he showed me a sign I'd work hard to be the man he wanted me to be. Truth was God had already showed me that sign. I was begging God for a gift I had selfishly squandered because I couldn't put her feelings first. She owed me nothing and I owed her an apology. The night after I was arrested I picked up my phone and called her. I remember asking Nicole, "Do you remember me? I just called to say I'm sorry. I was wrong. I never should have said what I said to you that night. I know you're probably seeing someone else and I don't even know if you want to talk to me or care to hear it but I'm sorry and I hope you can forgive me. I hope we can be friends." I honestly expected Nicole to curse me out and hang up the phone but instead she said "Richard I've already forgiven you," and asked me how I'd been? I told her I hadn't been the best. I was depressed and needed a friend and on that night we talked. I still can't believe she even answered the phone. With a tear in my eye as I write, God thank you for answering my prayers!

We started to work our way back into each other's lives but it wasn't an instant process nor should it have been. I had hurt my friend and I knew it. I was just happy to be reconnected with her. I felt as though a sense of stability had come back into my life. I knew through it all, my good days and my bad days, that I would have someone to talk with that cared about what I was going through and this time I promised myself that I would return the favor. Eventually we discussed the night we stopped speaking and what we'd both been through while living our separate lives. We talked about how in that year we both spiraled out of control for our own reasons. Talked about the men she dealt with and the women I dealt with, the moments of depression we'd both experienced. We talked our way back into each other's hearts. If those eleven months without Nicole in my life taught me anything it's that when the communication in a relationship dies, the relationship itself isn't far behind. So often when we're faced with problems in relationships; we'd rather take flight than fight. I thought it'd be easier to run from love but like Nicole always told me, "Nothing worth having comes easy."I've come to understand that I'm blessed and highly favored. For her to even take the time to hear and receive my apology was one thing, for her to trust me with her heart again was another completely. Yet here we were again almost two years after we had first met. It was January of 2008 now, and we'd finally decided that we were ready to be more than friends. Nicole and I had, "the conversation." We were now boyfriend and girlfriend. I let go of the guilt and pain I was feeling and embraced the second chance I'd been blessed with but I knew Nicole deserved more. Our relationship had a long way to go but we were talking again and that was a start. Open and honest communication between two parties is a vital component of any healthy relationship. The biggest factor in the break-up Nicole and I experienced was poor communication, mostly on my behalf and I knew that if I wanted us to work I'd have to do better.

* * *

How I Was Able To Forgive (Nicole)

As a child I was always taught that forgiveness was not for the other person but for your own peace of mind. I had to forgive Richard for his harsh words and reaction that night and while it may not have been easy, it was undoubtedly necessary. I knew he was hurting. The way we were hurting may have been different but the end result for each of us was unbearable pain and irrational decision making. Richard lashed out simply because he was unable to properly display his pain. I know now that he couldn't even process what I had told him. In that exact moment I was unable to rationalize his reaction because I simply thought he was being an insensitive, cold-hearted ass. It took time for me to calm down and allow my mind to do what's intended of it and to put my heart back in its proper place. As the weeks had gone by without us speaking I was able to reflect on the situation from a perspective other than my own and it was during that time of reflection I realized the severity of the situation and what exactly I had burdened Richard with. It wasn't that he didn't care in fact it was the total opposite. It was not an easy pill to swallow because honestly, it was easier for me to blame him for our hiatus and take absolutely no responsibility in the matter. However, doing so was getting us nowhere fast and I seemed to be spiraling to nowhere good even faster.

During one of the hardest periods in my life came one of my greatest lessons. I learned that being able to step outside of your emotions and consider someone else is not only mature but more importantly, it is beneficial because it aides in healing. Once I was able to process what had happened to me and properly deal with the trauma, I was then able to step back and consider what Richard may have been experiencing when he received the news and the helplessness that he was left to feel because he was unable to protect me. It did not happen instantly. I went through a time of serious self-destruction. I had temporarily become a cigarette smoking, serial dating, and robot like woman with a harsh and venomous tongue. I was hurting and I operated with two intentions; first, to hurt others second, to never be hurt again. I was also living by a reckless and callused mantra of 'life is short so live it to the fullest, regret nothing, throw caution to the wind and screw people because they are never what God created them to be, only what the Devil has convinced them to be.' One day a few months before Richard's call I looked at my reflection in the mirror and completely broke down. I saw this once beautiful woman aging fast, who's dignity was shrinking and her life growing out of control by the minute. I was becoming an insecure little girl reeking of naivety and quickly throwing away what self respect I had left. I was gaining weight, losing hair and battling depression. That day I hopped into the shower with the intent to cleanse my body, heart and soul.

As I showered I scrubbed my entire body until it stung with rawness. I stayed in there until I became an icebox from the water running cold. I fell to my knees crying; screaming and praying to a God I thought had forsaken me. It was in that moment that I realized God was always there! I was the one abandoning myself and the Lord too. After over an hour in the shower, I swaddled myself in a towel, laid in my bed soaking wet and drifted into the most peaceful sleep I had in years. When I awakened I ran to the mirror and this time I saw the woman I knew before the rape. I was glad to have her back and was ready to take back my life. I forgave myself for all the unjust punishment and blame. I forgave Richard for his reaction and I forgave my attacker for being the lost soul he was. More importantly I prayed that karma would spare his mother, sisters, aunts, cousins and daughters. I prayed that they would never have to reap from another man what he burdened me with. I also said a prayer for anyone who has ever had their body taken from them and asked God to remind them that their smile, their spirit, and their worth is theirs solely and no matter what happens no one can take those precious gifts away. They are not victims but victors who went through Hell and survived. I let go and I gave it to God!

Loving someone through their hurt is very tiresome but if you feel they're worth it then you have to lace up your boots, roll up your pants, do the work and march through the storm to get to the sunshine. Besides, in life you must be willing to give all that you wish to receive. We're all human and can at times be difficult to deal with, as the saying goes "Do unto others as you would have them do unto you," Easier said than done, but certainly words to live by.

10 Tips On Healthy Communication

Throughout our relationship and over the course of our marriage, we've adopted several methods that have helped us to better communicate in conversations with each other. I hope that these ten, tips on communication are helpful to you!

1.) **Never assume, Always ask.** In important discussions with your partner, try not to assume you know what it is they mean. If you're unsure of what your partner meant, it's better to ask than to remain uncertain.

2.) **Speak with love.** Often we speak harshest to the person(s) we love most because we take for granted they'll always be around to listen. Be mindful of how you're speaking to your loved ones, and do your best to speak lovingly to and about them.

3.) **Listen to understand, not to argue.** Often in a heated discussion, we find ourselves listening only to prove our next point rather than listening in order to understand. Do your best to comprehend what it is your partner is saying, and try to avoid listening solely for the purpose of countering your next point of argument.

4.) **Don't be afraid to go to bed 'angry.'** This is unpopular advice and goes against traditional wisdom; going to bed, angry isn't always a bad thing. If the couple is mature enough to agree to revisit the issue at an agreed upon later time, and can agree to kiss, say, "I love you," and offer each other a sincere, "goodnight." There is nothing wrong with a couple going to bed angry and waiting for cooler heads and calmer hearts to prevail.

5.) **Be mindful of your tone in heated discussions.** A loud argumentative tone, often only increases the tension in the room between everyone involved and causes individuals to shut down. Ensure both parties feel heard and respected; even during disagreements. Monitor your tone and do your best to keep things peaceful.

6.) **Try not to interrupt your partner.** This is one many struggle with, but interrupting your mate makes them feel irrelevant. When you interrupt, you give your mate the impression you do not value their opinion. Do your best not to interject while your significant other is talking.

7.) **Sandwich your criticisms.** When criticizing your mate it's sometimes best to offer a positive statement, then your criticism, followed by another positive statement. For example, "I love you dear. You're an excellent provider and very caring. However, I would really appreciate it if you helped out around the house more often. There's more here than I can do alone and I need your help. I know you're busy, and I thank you for all you do. Can you work on this for me?" *Sandwich your criticisms.*

8.) **Apologize.** If you've said something that has offended your mate, acknowledge the statement and correct it.

9.) **Never be afraid to agree to disagree.** No two people will agree on everything and it should never be expected. What should be expected is that the two parties can disagree with one another respectfully.

10.) **After every discussion, say "I love you."** Nothing is promised. Never pass up an opportunity to say, "I love you..." to those you care about.

We're not therapist or relationship experts. These are just some things that have helped us to better communicate with each other.

CHAPTER THREE

Reconnecting

By January of 2008 Nicole and I were finally starting to get past the year we had spent apart but it was not an easy process. We argued plenty. I found myself questioning her every move during the time we were separated which was wrong of me. I didn't see it as wrong at the time but for some selfish reason I felt she owed me an explanation for the things she'd done while we weren't speaking. My twenty-four year old male ego was hurt that she wasn't "stuck" on me and instead of admitting that to her openly I hid it behind accusations of her "wrong" behavior. To her credit she put up with my insecurities and I have to believe that she could see I was insecure, but also that I was genuinely concerned and in love with her and just didn't know how to show it. Yet no matter how much we argued I was thankful we were talking again. She made it clear to me that if she was going to invest her time into our relationship she needed me to clarify what we were to each other. If we were friends then we could be just that and see other people. If we wanted to be a couple then we needed to be exclusive.

It was during those conversations that I began reflecting on where my life was at the time. I was twenty-four years old beginning my second year of Graduate School, while working as a Paraprofessional and coaching a youth basketball team. I was busy but as busy as I may have been I was unhappy and unfulfilled. I found myself struggling to find happiness because none of the things I was doing in my life were things I saw myself doing forever. I never saw myself as a teacher but people around me told me I'd make a good one so I pursued it. I enjoyed coaching basketball but I wasn't being paid for it and was barely making enough money to survive on a day to day basis so I didn't know if that could continue. I was flunking out of school because I had stopped going. I was confused, lonely and depressed because I had no idea in the world what it was I wanted outside of a relationship with Nicole. We'd known each other two years, and for eleven months of that time we hadn't spoken. We hadn't laid eyes on each other since that night we met. How could we know that what we shared was real? Not long after her and I reconnected I received a promotion at work. I went to attend the new hire meeting and during the signing of paperwork was given a life insurance policy to fill out. It was at that moment I began to ask myself what my life really meant. I was turning twenty-five soon and I sat in that meeting realizing I had no one to leave anything to. I had no children, no serious girlfriend in my opinion at the time, but I had Nicole. I sat there for a minute thinking about how I was in love with her, how we'd shared so much with one another. How she'd been such a source of comfort for me in the times I needed it most and how she was reliable. Nicole was my best friend.

In two years there was never a time I called her that she didn't answer or call right back. Since Nicole and I were an online relationship my parents would never understand why I loved her so much. It wouldn't make sense to them, hell it barely made sense to me. Something hit me that day that I couldn't explain but at that moment I felt as though I had a responsibility to take care of the woman I loved. As a friend I had abandoned her when she needed me most. As a potential lover I avoided commitment at every turn and yet she continued to stand by my side and give me her time, friendship and love. If I were to have died she deserved to know and the only way I could have guaranteed that happened was to sign her name to my life insurance policy. I thought to myself if I were to pass away maybe she could use that little bit of money to make herself happy in the same way she helped to make me happy. She deserved it. That was the first time I think I actually felt like I deserved Nicole. Before then I hadn't done anything to deserve her love. I never told her that I named her my beneficiary. I didn't want to speak death over my life. But it wasn't long after that day in the new hire meeting that I asked Nicole if she wanted to arrange a visit. Finally, after two years of speaking online and over the phone we were ready to meet in person. Nicole had some extra money saved and she paid for my plane ticket to Ohio. I chose a weekend I was getting paid so I could pay for dinner and everything else we did once I landed. At last our situation was actually becoming a relationship and honestly I was nervous because I didn't know if I was ready. However, I knew I didn't want to let the opportunity pass so I put my fear to the side and boarded a plane headed to Columbus, OH to see the woman I loved.

I landed in Ohio at about 8:00 Saturday night in late February 2008. I got off that plane looking a mess and thinking back I couldn't have made a worse first impression. My hair wasn't freshly cut and I wasn't dressed on the plane like I was going to be headed out that evening. I wasn't dressed like I was really meeting a woman I loved and cared about for the first time. I walked up to Nicole and we hugged, but something didn't feel quite right. She told me later that she was a little disappointed because after so many years and so much time invested she expected me to come to her at my "best." I completely understand why today as her husband I should have taken my responsibility as her boyfriend seriously. I expected my lady to give me a maximum effort while only delivering the bare minimum of myself. In relationships we often do that without realizing it. We expect the best out of our mates while making no real effort to provide them with anything besides our worst. I can honestly say that I wasn't coming to impress Nicole and I should have been. I allowed fear to be the reason I didn't give my best because I was scared my best wasn't good enough. I was sabotaging my relationship before it ever got started attempting to push her away because I was afraid she wouldn't want the best of me.

Meeting new people is hard for me. I grow quiet and nervous around folks I don't really know well. Over the years I've grown to appreciate how comfortable Nicole makes me in those situations when the two of us are together. After our embrace we walked through the airport to gather my bags and at that time I asked her if she wanted to get a hotel room for the weekend because I wasn't comfortable staying at her mothers' house. She had recently moved back home but assured me that it was alright for the two of us to spend the weekend there together. We grabbed my things, left the Airport and drove about twenty minutes to where Nicole lived. We talked about our day. Nicole had been at her grandmother's funeral and was grieving; I had worked all day and had been traveling, so we were both physically and mentally exhausted. When we pulled up to the house I grabbed my bags and Nicole escorted me inside. At the door her mother greeted us, gave me a big hug and said, "Welcome home." To this day that's one of the warmest sentiments anyone has ever expressed to me, especially considering the day they'd had and I'm very thankful for it. That was my first time meeting the woman who'd become my mother-in-law. She didn't know me, didn't know how I'd treat her or her daughter but she said, "Welcome home." That spoke volumes to me about the type of person Nicole was. The only people I'd ever known to be that genuinely welcoming to strangers was my grandmother and her older sisters. They'd welcome any and everyone with open arms. Meeting Nicole's mother for that first time I couldn't help but think of the four women who played such integral parts in my life growing up. I thought to myself, "This is rare,. Nicole really is good people."

I placed my bags in Nicole's room and then the two of us freshened up and discussed what we were going to eat for dinner. We decided on Italian. Nicole ordered chicken, I ordered seafood pasta and we shared calamari; which has become a theme in our relationship. Whenever we go to a new restaurant we share calamari. It takes us back to memories of our first night together. It's one of our little, things. We've learned over time that it's the little things that help to build a bond between a couple. Those inside jokes or special moments only the two of you know about, calamari was our first "little thing." Dinner was a beautiful time and as the night went on I began feeling like I had just seen her yesterday. It's strange going on a first date two years after getting to know someone so intimately. We may not have known each other in the physical sense but we were well acquainted mentally. Once I began to realize that the physical person I was sitting across from was the same woman I fell in love with over the phone I couldn't get enough of her but that didn't change the awkward feelings in the air that I knew the both of us were feeling.

We weren't really sure if we were a couple and if so, what kind of couple were we? So we talked. Nicole made her relationship expectations clear and that obviously wasn't the first time we'd had the conversation but there was something different about talking in person. I think that's why everything about that first visit was so uncomfortable. What stands out to me most about it years later are all the ways I mishandled such an important occasion. Nicole told me how she felt that night over dinner. She explained that when I first laid eyes on her I looked almost disappointed as if maybe I wasn't attracted to her because of her weight gain. Nothing was further from the truth because I honestly think my wife is gorgeous but I can see why she got that impression. I didn't take time to represent myself or my relationship like it was serious to me but expected her to take me seriously and for that I was wrong. Relationships are about reciprocity and I was failing to reciprocate the efforts Nicole made for us to be together yet expected her to overlook my lack of effort and continue to give me her best. I was selfish and my selfish nature was impacting the woman I loved. I needed to do better.

After finishing dinner Nicole and I left the restaurant headed home to her place and during the ride the conversation of whether or not we should have sex came up. We'd both been tested recently, were both clean, and Nicole was on birth control. We discussed whether or not we should use condoms and decided against it at my urging, which was wrong of me. I should have never allowed Nicole to feel pressured out of her decisions, especially sexually. My insistence against using condoms said to her, "I have to have sex with him this weekend," When nothing was further from the truth but I allowed her to believe that lie because I believed it benefited my "needs." I was lonely and felt like sex was a need when it wasn't. The only thing her and I needed to do that weekend was get to know one another better and my fear of embracing a real relationship clouded my better judgment. Instead of having sex we should have been having nothing but in-depth conversations. I selfishly persisted in my attempts to sleep with Nicole until she did it only to shut her boyfriend up. I could feel her discomfort throughout the entire time. There was no passion, no intimacy; it wasn't what I wanted because she didn't want it but it took me too long to come to that realization. Hindsight is 20/20 especially when you weren't thinking with the right head initially.

Many times in relationships we do things because we feel obligated to please our partner and that is very unhealthy. Nicole only slept with me that first trip because she felt as though it would make me happy and I allowed her to believe that because at the time I felt like if she loved me she'd have sex with me. I was confusing lust with love. The reality was if I had loved her the way she deserved I'd have never asked or allowed her to feel obligated to commit her body to me when I hadn't even taken on the obligation to mentally and spiritually connect to her. Our relationship was too new, too uncertain and I had not yet proved I was deserving of intimacy in even the most basic of ways. In relationships couples need to be honest with one another about their willingness and readiness to move forward, whether it is in their relationship and/or the bedroom. Both parties should feel comfortable and never forced and my failure to recognize Nicole's true feelings would help to cast a shadow over our future. I was sabotaging our love with my destructive behavior and Nicole was enabling me to a certain extent which was hurting her and our relationship. While we may have finally laid to rest our issues about dating, we'd stumbled upon the realization that dating one another would take as much work as courting each other had; if not more. However, despite the difficulties we faced our relationship was progressing and for that I was thankful, even if I didn't know how to show it.

✶✶✶

Do Things At Your Discretion (Nicole)

That weekend was truly eye-opening for me. I realized that I had a mentality I assumed all men had. I deemed sex as the most evident way to prove you cared for a significant other. I will always recall the heaviness of the first time Richard and I had sex. Nothing about it felt organic. I didn't feel forced by him but I did in fact feel pressured. I felt self imposed pressure. I had fallen victim to the notion that if you love someone you give all of yourself. In my heart I knew I should've waited but my mind was telling me "what you don't do, another woman will." It was in that moment that a harsh honesty swept over my heart. I realized that this was not the first time that I'd used sex to imitate emotion. I questioned how many other women were having sex for that exact reason? Well, after many conversations with numerous female friends, I found out it was more common than not. Not only did I learn women were using sex to express emotion but sex was also often the culprit in creating emotions when there was really none there. It was a vicious cycle that I was determined to end whether Richard and I worked out or not. I wanted to live every aspect of life that I could control, on my terms. While I wish we could travel back in time and do the episode entirely different, I learned an invaluable lesson. I learned that sex with no love was just sex but love without premature sex was the purest love there is!

Whenever entering into a relationship, be sure to do things at your discretion and comfort level. If you are not careful and relinquish total power to your partner you can bet your bottom dollar that you'll become resentful of them eventually. I am blessed that I was able to revisit the occurrence via conversation and everything panned out. Once I expressed the awkwardness I was feeling that evening, he too expressed that he was not totally comfortable or even convinced that either of us were ready. That initial conversation opened the lines of communication more than we ever thought possible. Oddly enough, most adults can partake in sexual activity yet squirm with embarrassment at even the thought of discussing it. Having a very in depth conversation about sex taught the two of us a lot about one another's sexual needs but more importantly it taught us how to read each other's context clues. I know in relationships there is no mind reading but there is plenty reading of body language.

The Sex Talk *(Richard)*

So many couples talk about the act of sex but rarely do couples talk about the true intimacy the act of sex requires. Having sexual intercourse with your mate is different from making love. I'd engaged in sexual activity before but it wasn't until I slept with Nicole the first time that I realized I had no idea how to make love. I felt as though Nicole caved into the pressure my vibe put off. I had made jokes about us having sex that night before we'd even had dinner. I honestly was joking, but I never took into account Nicole didn't know that. She'd heard me joke before, but she'd never seen it. She wasn't accustomed to it. My disposition during our initial visit led to us having sex before either of us was comfortable. We let the length of time we'd been friends' play too much of a part in what happened on that first night we spent together. "We've known each other two years, and this is what people do..." ran through both of our heads. We were wrong. What we should have done was ask questions. We asked each other "are you sleeping with someone else?" We asked, "When's the last time you were tested?" We asked about birth control and condoms but we never asked about our emotions. Couples often jump into sex without discussing the act first which can be a devastating mistake. As awkward as the conversations may seem, they need to be shared between significant others.

5 Things To Discuss With Your Partner Before Engaging In Sex The First Time

1.) How often do you expect/need sex? Do you use sex as an escape or to, "self-medicate", when going through difficulties? What is a healthy sex life to you?

2.) Has sexual dissatisfaction ever caused you to end a relationship? If you were dissatisfied with our sex life, how would we handle it?

3.) What is foreplay to you? Does it consist of cuddling and quiet conversation? Or do you like to get straight to kissing, touching, oral sex, etc. the moment we decide we're going to be intimate?

4.) What type of sex do you enjoy? Do you expect rough sex, passionate sex, "freaky" sex, or does how we feel at the time dictate the "type" of sex we have? Or do you always expect to have the same "type" of sex?

5.) What type of environment are you most comfortable in when it comes to sex? Are you a private, bedroom only person? Are you adventurous and like to try new things?

These were the types of conversations Nicole and I should have engaged in prior to having sex. Avoidance led to years of misunderstandings about what intimacy really meant to us. We encourage couples to have a deeper conversation about sex with one another. Never feel afraid or embarrassed to get naked in front of your partner; emotionally naked that is. Before you get naked physically, get naked emotionally. The moment you and your partner have a true understanding of what intimacy is in your relationship is the moment you move from having sex, to making love.

Our suggestion: each individual in addition to the provided questions, create their own list with questions that are of great importance to them and make a copy to answer along with your partner. Next, sit down answer and discuss each other's questions including your own questions openly and honestly, with dialog and clarity being your only objective. Be sure to document both sets of questions and answers. Store them in a secure place to revisit, re-read and even re-answer if necessary throughout your relationship. Always remember that who you are today is not who you'll be tomorrow if you live a life of evolution and maturation and the same goes for your partner. Keeping this notion at the forefront of your mind allows you to stay understanding of the person you fell in love with, while respecting and appreciating the person they're becoming. We have formatted the questions to be answered in an open dialogue between you and your partner.

CHAPTER FOUR

Yet Another Chance

When I returned home from that first visit with Nicole I began to take stock of my life in ways I'd never really done before. We were finally a couple but the 400 miles separating us was still an issue and I was in no financial position to close the gap. As soon as the happiness of new love had come it had gone and it had been replaced with feelings of inadequacy. What woman wants a man who can't provide for her? We knew that we couldn't maintain a long distance relationship much longer so we began discussing plans on who'd move. We debated which location was better; Columbus, Ohio, or Rochester, New York? At first I went hard for her to move to Rochester because I had a job, was in school and to me it made complete sense on the surface. Nicole reminded me she knew the truth beneath the surface. I don't know how she does it but somehow she could see straight through me and I began to realize how much of a blessing an attentive and caring woman could be for a man. From miles away she could see that I was pretending everything was fine when something was clearly wrong. Around this time our conversations began to get deeper and quite honestly I didn't know our conversations could go any further but they did. She began to ask me if teaching was truly what I wanted to do for the rest of my life? I told her no, I wanted to be an athletic director at a division one college or general manager for an NBA team. That's when Nicole asked me, "Do you think teaching is the best route to that career?" I sat there one night pondering that question. Nicole had raised a question I wasn't ready for. I was a man with dreams and no plan and a man with a dream and no plan is destined to fail. Then here comes this woman who cares enough about my happiness to help me realize that a dream wasn't enough. I lacked purpose and Nicole didn't give me a purpose but cared enough to help me focus on what I was overlooking. She sharpened my sight. I was living someone else's dreams hoping that I'd achieve my goals. That was a recipe for disaster. Looking back at that time in my life I thank her for caring when I truly needed it.

Weeks passed by as March turned into April and Nicole and I were beginning to speak more frequently on the phone. The majority of our conversations in the past had taken place late at night or in the wee-hours of the morning but since our first visit we had begun talking regularly during the afternoon. As we became closer I broke down and told her that I had dropped out of school since we last saw one another but hadn't yet told my parents. My mother was so proud of my accomplishments in school and I went back mainly because she insisted on it. My father was always indifferent to it in general, he was proud of what I'd already accomplished. It was during this time that Nicole began to realize I didn't exactly have the best relationship with my parents and don't get me wrong I love them dearly; we just don't always have the best relationship. She and I began to get heavily involved with one another during a period in my life where my parents and I were going through it. Since I knew my mother wouldn't react well to me dating a woman I essentially met online I chose not to tell my parents about my girlfriend. Nicole questioned me as to why I didn't tell them about her. It concerned her that we were getting serious yet no one close to me knew she existed. I completely understood her argument and knew it was a valid one but my fear once again over-ruled my better judgment. Instead of making the woman I loved known to my family I persuaded her to allow herself to remain hidden because it would make my life easier. Nicole and I had a very unique relationship that I didn't feel like my parents could understand. We were an internet couple and many people just don't really understand how someone can find true love online. Seems impossible at least, desperate at worst. I allowed the fear of how others would view us to compromise my love and for that I was wrong. I would have to get over the fear of what others may say about our relationship in order to love her properly and I knew that but wasn't ready. Then life happened.

It was late April when I received a disturbing phone call at work. It was Nicole's friend Mya. I knew the call had to be important because Nicole had my work number but never used it before and for her to have someone else call me on her behalf meant it was an emergency. The news I received that afternoon would change life as I knew it. I walked out into the hallway to take the phone call. I don't remember the conversation but I'll never forget the news. The phone was given to Nicole. She was in the hospital after suffering through a miscarriage earlier in the day. Neither of us knew that the visit we'd had together several weeks earlier had resulted in a pregnancy. April of 2008 is when our Angel baby went to Heaven or at least that's what I told myself to get through it. Nicole had just suffered through a miscarriage and I don't know what hurt more? The miscarriage, me being unable to comfort the woman I loved through an agonizing moment, or the fact that she had gotten pregnant while having sex with me only because she felt obligated to. I was a wreck emotionally but tried my best to hold it together for her. I got off work and went home. A few hours would pass before Nicole called. We talked again and during the conversation all kinds of questions began to pour through my head. I asked myself could this really be happening to me or was Nicole lying? Was she trying to see how emotionally attached to her I was? Was Nicole trying to see if I was willing to commit? I hated the fact that those questions were pouring through my mind. I never saw her as that type of woman and I felt wrong for even assuming those types of things about her. I went back and forth about whether or not to ask Nicole did she really miscarry? That's a very insensitive question to ask a woman and I never wanted her to think I didn't care. At the same time I was questioning her, I also began to question myself. If she hadn't miscarried, and that phone call was to let me know she was pregnant, what kind of father would I have been? Was I ready for the responsibilities that I had avoided in my life for so long? Could I hold down a steady job which provided enough income for my family? Could I treat the mother of my child with love and respect? Could I be in a committed relationship for the rest of my life? I'd never wanted a "baby-momma," I've always wanted a wife but was I ready for marriage? As I sat around asking myself these questions I began realizing how wrong it was of me to question her. Through the years we'd known each other she had proven to be stronger in the love we shared than I was. I felt ashamed because if she wouldn't have miscarried I'm not sure I'd have been man enough to be the man she required. I wasn't sure if I'd be man enough to be the father my child deserved. I will never forget the doubt that ran through my mind. I started looking at the path my life was truly taking and for once I was able to admit that I needed a change.

I realized that I was insecure. How could I be a strong father and/or husband if I wasn't sure of who I was and what I wanted as a man? Did I want to coach basketball? Did I want to be a writer? I'd always loved writing and always said I wanted to write a book but I never gave it a serious try. I began to realize I was becoming the man I'd always said I never wanted to be. That man who quit everything he started before he ever really gave a true effort. The man who was too afraid to try because he was certain he'd fail. I was that man and I had to ask myself was a man who was unable to finish anything he started ready to commit to a relationship with a woman who deserved certainty? Was I ready to provide Nicole with the stability she deserved? I gathered up the courage to ask her as politely as I could whether or not she was really pregnant? She told me she expected the question and realized it wasn't unreasonable to ask given the circumstances of our relationship. She'd kept her discharge papers from the hospital because she expected that question. I honestly let all the questions go about our Angel baby because the fact remains that Nicole never used that baby as a "trap" so to speak. That phone call wasn't for her, it was for me. She knew how much I'd always wanted children and felt as though I deserved to know that she had just miscarried our child. She also needed my support emotionally as a lover and friend and for once in our long, complicated relationship, I was there for her.

We cried over the phone that night about our present and dreamed about our futures. With each passing day it seemed like the relationship Nicole and I shared was moving from just some fantasy to an almost impossible reality. That miscarriage made me look at myself and take stock of life in a way I had never done before. It shouldn't take a tragic event to make a person see the light but so often it does. Slowly but surely the conversation that night turned to whether or not Nicole and I would get engaged because emotional nights often have a way of bringing about serious conversations like that. It was an exciting yet scary time for the both of us. In the days leading up to her graduation it became clear I wouldn't be able to attend and I felt horrible. I knew all the obstacles Nicole faced during college and I wanted to be there for her. My car had died earlier that year back in January and I was unable to get a new one. I had no affordable way to reach Ohio to see her walk the stage. I honestly wanted nothing more than to be there to show my love and support especially after the miscarriage she suffered, but once again I felt like I was letting her down. Nicole assured me that she understood and wasn't upset. She realized we were in a unique situation that was hard on the both of us. She was proving to be a stabilizing force in my life and I knew that I needed to make amends for the mistakes I'd made in our past. I'd made a lot of promises to her and through tragedy I came to realize that talk was cheap. I was determined to show her that I was a better man than I had previously displayed.

May of 2008. Nicole made plans to visit me in Rochester. I didn't ask, and honestly didn't expect her to but she decided to use some of her graduation money to visit me. I wanted her to do something nice for herself because she definitely deserved it. Considering how unimpressive I was in our first meeting I promised myself I'd show her a better time than I did on my visit to Ohio. She'd just graduated from college and she deserved something special. Our future looked promising but was not without hardships. For a long time I believed that the relationship we shared would get easier as time passed when in reality life became harder because it became more important. Things that once meant little began to mean the world to me. Responsibilities began to increase and with those came added fear and uncertainty, which is why I believe I tried so hard for so long not to give my all in a relationship. I was beginning to realize that the hardships and responsibilities I was trying to avoid were the things that truly made life worth living. I was beginning to learn that I couldn't claim love without owning the duties that true love requires like patience, respect, honesty, trust, fidelity and compassion. I was eager to show Nicole that I was serious about our future.

***

True Love Is Far From A Fairy Tale (Nicole)

Hard times test your relationship but overcoming those hard times strengthens the bond. Going through such an event without Richard was rough but luckily I wasn't alone. I was with Mya, a close college friend and she stayed there with me the entire time. The first conversation following the bad news was rough. I was drained physically, emotionally, mentally and in equal amounts of pain in each of those categories. Regardless, I collected the strength and energy to have the conversation because I knew speaking to Richard was the right thing to do. I had yet again dropped a very heavy bomb on him and was certain he had questions. When he asked if I had really miscarried I honestly wasn't offended because I was just as surprised by what happened as he was. Hell, I was in total disbelief. I was on the shot! How could I have miscarried? I didn't even know I was pregnant. Why was I so emotionally hurt, it wasn't like I even knew to have an attachment? Was I hurt from the actual loss or the notion that the miscarriage was somehow my fault? All these thoughts were running through my mind.

Richard has been my person, the one that I can crumble around and still be viewed solid as a rock. We were there for each other and through each hardship our relationship still seemed to be flourishing. However, the reality remained; we weren't ready for a child, so I guess what is said is true, "All things happen for a reason." I learned in that instance that being strong and independent are not the same as being self-sufficient. I was CAPABLE of being all three but I didn't need to be. In a marriage you need to allow yourself to display vulnerability. In marriage you exchange your total independence for interdependency, leaning on each other to make it work. Accepting your weaknesses makes both the relationship and the individual stronger. I don't need my husband to survive but I'm not afraid to need my husband through survival.

Reveal Your Weaknesses To Strengthen Your Relationship
(Richard)

There is strength in being vulnerable with the one you love. Many times in a relationship people attempt to put on a façade as if they're always in control for their partner because they want to appear strong. I've learned that in a relationship the ability to be transparent with the one you love is the embodiment of strength. For a long time I tried to act as though I had everything together because I worried that if Nicole saw uncertainty or weakness I would not be attractive to her anymore. My attempts at being strong were hindering the growth of our relationship and I didn't realize that until the miscarriage. Having to share fears of inadequacy in being able to provide for her gave her the insight she needed to be the lover she promised me she'd always be. Your partner can only be supportive effectively if you're open to receiving their support.

It felt safe keeping Nicole at a distance because the further she was from my heart the less she could hurt me, or at least that's what I was telling myself up until that tragic moment. Attempting to run from my feelings was unhealthy and hurting our relationship. With the loss of our child I began to realize that life was too short to be taken for granted and if I loved Nicole the way I claimed to, she needed to know exactly how I felt about her, myself and our relationship. A couple has to be honest about their feelings in order to thrive. Sharing with Nicole my fear of fatherhood her response to it was comforting because she wasn't ready to be a mother either. We were uncertain what the future held but felt empowered by the knowledge that we were willing to face that uncertain future together. There is strength in being vulnerable with the one you love. Couples have to make a commitment to being transparent with their feelings about life, love, work, parenthood, friends, temptations, failures and successes. Nothing can be off-limits between a couple headed towards the altar. Be open, be honest and be compassionate so that your mate feels comfortable doing the same.

CHAPTER FIVE

A Natural Progression

Looking back on the spring of 2008 I've realized that it was the time in our relationship when Nicole and I had what I like to call, "The conversations which lead to marriage." She and I did not decide to get married on a whim although it probably seemed that way to our friends and families. Over the course of two years I had truly grown to consider Nicole my best-friend and more importantly we'd fallen deeply in love with one another. We were having the marriage conversation at the right time in our relationship but like many men I was fighting it all the way even though I knew marrying her was the right decision. When I needed support she provided it. When I needed love she gave it. When I required attention I received it from her. When I needed comfort, I called on Nicole. For the first time in my life I felt strong enough and more importantly loved enough to be vulnerable. Her love gave me the courage to face my biggest fears, life-long commitment and being worthy of true love.

Here we were sitting on the phone every night casually talking about moving and being together and then on one night in particular Nicole said, "I want to get married September 5th, 2009." I suggested a 2012 wedding date and she rejected because as she said she wasn't interested in being a six year girlfriend. She came with her argument and I have to be honest, it was convincing. She emphasized that we had been involved for two years, which at the time didn't make sense to me because for one of the years we'd known each other, her and I didn't speak. Nicole reminded me that the break-up we'd experienced was my fault and not hers. She'd spent two years with her heart vested into me and was unwilling to continue to do so for much longer without the certainty of commitment. If I was unwilling to commit to her in a reasonable time frame we could continue to be friends but eventually she would begin to see other people and wouldn't hold it against me if I did the same.

Nicole was making it quite clear that she was willing to walk away from our relationship if I was unwilling to walk into a commitment. Prior to meeting her I had always told myself I would seriously consider marriage if after being with a woman for two years she and I were really considering settling down together. It seemed like I had finally found what I was looking for but now that I'd found it I was terrified. I was scared of what the future would hold and whether or not I'd measure up to Nicole's expectations of what a husband should be. My entire life I doubted myself because I felt like I let the people around me down and I didn't want Nicole to be the latest in a long line of victims. I was self destructive, argumentative, and hot tempered. I was reclusive, moody and impulsive. I harbored so many issues I felt made me unlovable yet for some reason Nicole remained by my side. She remained on my mind even when she wasn't in my life. She clung to my heart even without us being around one another but I knew that if I continued to string our relationship along I risked losing her. She and I would discuss marriage almost every day before her first visit to Rochester and the message was becoming very clear, she wanted commitment from me and was unwilling to accept anything less. I'd been served notice.

In the meantime I anxiously awaited Nicole's arrival. I took two days off from work and planned out some things for us to do together. I was finally able to spend time with her after that disastrous first meeting in Ohio. It was Monday, May 5th, 2008. Nicole arrived in Rochester around 2:00pm in the afternoon and picked me up from work after making the eight hour drive to New York. As always she looked picture perfect. Her hair, makeup and wardrobe were stylish yet classy like something out of a movie. I used to say to myself that I wanted an elegant, intelligent and well put together lady on my arm. Nicole's values, class and professionalism were very attractive to me. She embodied the essence of the woman I always saw myself with. When I told her I got off work around 2:50pm and she was waiting for me as soon as I walked out of the door of my job waiting there dressed to the nines I was like, "That's impressive, do your thing baby!" It was in that moment I knew what she expected of me that first meeting, she expected my best. She came to me at that day at her best and set an example for our relationship I still aspire to live up to. Teal dress, gold sandals with gold accessories to match, natural makeup and she wore her hair down. Her hair was thick, long and flowing, she was so beautiful. For the first time in forever I was truly having a great day. I considered taking the entire week off from work, but I'm glad I didn't. I would need those few remaining days in a month or so, although I didn't know that then. We left my job and stopped by my parents' house to pick up my things. No one was home so Nicole didn't get an opportunity to meet them and honestly I was glad. I wasn't ready for her to meet my family yet because I was worried about how the meeting may go. I gathered my things, packed a bag and we left my parents house and headed for the hotel. We stopped by a Chinese restaurant along the way to grab some takeout. After such a long day I knew Nicole needed to rest so I didn't plan for us to do anything that night. We arrived at the hotel and Nicole checked us in while I unpacked the car. We settled into the room and began our much awaited week together. On my visit to see her we spent less than forty-eight hours with each other so I wanted to make the best of our time. I didn't want to just spend it lying up in the hotel night after night watching television. I wanted to give my girlfriend a memorable week.

I felt bad because I felt like Nicole was blowing her graduation money on seeing me. I had a little cash in my pocket but wasn't getting paid until that upcoming Friday so I couldn't really treat her to a good time the way I wanted without us splitting the tab. A lot of women wouldn't have been willing to dip into their purse and pay for a trip to visit their out-of-town boyfriend and I knew that. I was grateful and had no question in my mind that she was special. I also knew that she deserved to be shown the best time I could offer her. I wanted to date her in a way she'd never forget. I knew we only had five days together but I wanted to create memories we could hold onto. I was honestly a little depressed I still had to go to work that week but my heart was set on leaving a lasting impression on the woman I loved, so I shook my feelings off and tried to make everything about her. Nicole deserved to be celebrated for her hard work. I was proud of her graduating because I knew how much she had been through on her journey towards a degree. I didn't want to ruin her memory of graduation by leaving a bad taste in her mouth like I did the last time we were together. I didn't know if her and I would make it as a couple but I knew that she deserved to smile, so I made it my goal to leave one on her face.

She and I talked a lot that evening. I told her what my work schedule would be. I would leave the hotel everyday at 7am and be back no later than 3:30pm to pick her up so we could go out on a date. I told her I could take Tuesday and Wednesday off like I had taken off Thursday and Friday, but she told me not to. Nicole said, "No, go to work because it'll feel sort of like real life you know? When you come back to the room I'll be dressed and ready to go out for the evening and we can relax." I liked the way Nicole thought. I always loved her perspective. It was so different from any other woman I'd ever met. The way Nicole sees the world inspires me to think deeper. I always wanted to be married before meeting her but I never really thought about what being married would feel like. She and I talked for hours that night. I remember the two of us dreaming together. The first visit we argued but this time we dreamed together and it felt completely different. Nicole talked about her time working for an independent music label and I told her that I always dreamed of turning poems I had written into songs. We dreamed. No plans were made just dreams shared and it felt intimate. We told each other things we had never shared with anyone else while we ate, relaxed and watched some television.

That night Nicole and I made love and I don't use the term loosely because I'd never made love before. I thought I had made love before but then I realized what I had experienced was sex because the women I experienced it with either didn't love me or weren't loved by me. Sometimes a combination of both but that night with Nicole was entirely different from even our first time together. Our first time should have never happened the way it did. We could feel the fear of the unknown between us yet proceeded anyway because we felt obligated to. This meeting was different. From the moment Nicole arrived it felt like seeing a long lost love. We could feel our relationship evolving and growing more serious. The two years of friendship carried out in an internet chat room, instant messages and late night phone calls had become real. We were still in a long distance relationship but we no longer felt like we were just an internet fantasy. Nicole and I finally felt like a couple. That first visit felt like a long blind date honestly. Like I had to impress her or else she wouldn't find me attractive anymore. This time I felt certain. We had visited with one another and she liked me enough to give it another chance and for that I was grateful because I didn't feel like I deserved it. I listened to her talk for two years, yet never heard her. Nicole is a survivor of sexual assault. In the past I've called her a victim never realizing that calling the woman I love a victim only victimizes her more and that's not what she needs from me. She is a survivor who deserves my compassion not a victim who deserves pity and definitely not a lady who deserves to be pressured.

When we finished making love that night I held her close and made sure to tell her that I loved her. I could feel for the first time that Nicole was truly comfortable around me. I thought about everything she trusted me with. What I learned that first night we made love is that listening wasn't enough. I learned that just loving Nicole wasn't enough. She was in love with me and I needed to be in love with her for our relationship to work. The woman I loved deserved my patience. She deserved not to be rushed and that night as I fell asleep in bliss wrapped tightly in her arms I finally understood what being in love meant. There were many things in my life I wasn't sure of but I was sure I wanted to marry Nicole Singleton. That first night she was in Rochester sealed the deal. This was the woman who was going to be my wife and she deserved nothing less than the best I had to offer. For the first time I stopped listening to what Nicole said and started hearing what she really meant. That night I went to bed happy. Not because I had just made love, but because I had just realized I was in love. I felt blessed and highly favored to be lying peacefully in Nicole's arms as I drifted off to sleep. Our relationship seemed to be moving towards forever and the thought was comforting.

✳ ✳ ✳

Know Your Desires, Expectations And Worth (Nicole)

I had been through too much unwarranted and unwanted pain to willingly partake in any of my future hurt. I realized, remembered and reinvented who I was and I liked the new me. What I wanted out of life was non-negotiable and I was determined to remain unwavering and steadfast in my life and happiness. I thought I had it all figured out. I may have learned plenty about myself but a relationship involves two people. Needless to say I would later learn that the lessons had only begun.

Richard and I had become more than an idea. I was elated however, I was more scared than I had ever recalled being in life. I thought back to past relationships and my behavior. I had given so much of myself in the past only to end up in the same predicament; alone, confused, heartbroken and exhausted. I knew what I felt for Richard was stronger and more real than anything I'd experienced before but was I ready for another potentially disastrous relationship? It was odd, I was still in love with the idea of love yet afraid to experience it again, I had become cynical. I always thought I was the "better to have loved and lost, than to have never loved at all" type of woman but with each failed relationship I was becoming annoyed with optimism. I had become so accustomed to being single that I convinced myself that I wasn't the marrying type, so why even date seriously? I had many long conversations with myself about what I was feeling and why I was experiencing so much turmoil. I knew I loved him. I knew we were amazing friends. I knew I wanted him in my life, but at what capacity? Finally, I concluded that I would put my heart on the line and take the risk. Why not? With great risk, comes great reward. I was determined to make this time different and in order to do so I had to change one major thing...me. I decided I was no longer going to go with the flow. I was never again going to let a man establish my future by dictating what I did and didn't deserve. I knew I was "wife material" and if Richard didn't then it was time to throw in the towel.

Too often we women do all we think a man wants us to in order to earn him as the prize. Damn that, we're the prize and if you want us then prove it! I had given Richard my expectations along with the option to either adhere to them and receive all the glory that is me, or don't and regret it for the rest of his life! Time waits for no one, so why should I? I explained to him that I loved him and cherished having him in my life but if friends was all he was aiming for, so be it, let's make our status/title clear. I didn't want him to feel pressured into a relationship but I also didn't want him to think he could string me along. I was done giving away girlfriend/wife benefits with nothing in return other than self proclaimed titles and assumptions. I know we have all been there. We meet a person, develop some type of "situationship" and never address where the relationship is going. Before you know it you have been seeing this individual regularly and sleeping with them just as often, and they have yet to profess to you or anyone else that you're their significant other. When it is all said and done there is no one to blame but yourself, you willingly gave that person the reins and didn't bother to inquire about the destination. Major no-no!

Are You Just Hearing Your Mate, Or Do You Really Listen (Richard)

Listening to your mate is an integral component of a healthy, lasting relationship. Listening to someone you care for is showing love, but while you're listening ask yourself, "What am I listening for?" Are you listening just to respond and be heard? Are you listening solely to build your case for a better argument? Are you listening to poke holes in their statements? Or are you listening to your mate with the best interest of your relationship in mind? Often, people listen only to find ways to improve their own position. In a lasting relationship, partners have to take care to listen in such a way that their mate feels heard.

I've learned that a great way to hold yourself accountable for how you're listening to your partner is asking yourself how they feel. In deep conversations with the one you're in love with, the things we say often convey unsaid feelings. Sometimes a person will tell you they're feeling "ok" but you can hear "I'll be okay once we talk." If what you hear from your partner makes you uncertain about how they feel it's best to ask questions for clarity. If your partner tells you they're feeling "ok," and you feel that you hear otherwise, take a second to ask if they're sincere. If they tell you, "yes," reassure them that they can come to you at any time to talk if something is bothering them and that if all they need you to do is listen, you're there with closed mouth, open ears and a clear mind. Not to respond, not to build your case, not for selfish motives and finger wagging, but out of selfless love. At all times try your best to listen to your partner and hear what it is they really have to say.

CHAPTER SIX

True Love Commits

That next morning I woke up early, went into work. For once going into work was truly a joy because returning "home" was something to look forward to. I made it through the day with the biggest grin on my face because Nicole has that effect on me you know? I never smiled much before I met her. I never felt like I had something to smile about. My smile made me feel uncomfortable. Nicole left me with a smile and that said it all to me. I sat at work that day thinking of how I could do the same for her. A man has to make a dedicated effort to show the woman he loves how he feels about her. On my trip I made to Ohio a few weeks earlier, Nicole and I went out to dinner at an Italian Restaurant and the food was decent but it was a chain we'd both been to a million times before. I wanted to do something special so I decided I'd take her out to dinner at the nicest Italian restaurant in Rochester. I wrapped the day up at work and headed back to the hotel with a smile on my face.

I walked in and Nicole was ready for my arrival as she told me she would be the day before. Hair done, makeup flawless and dressed to impress;

on that day she was at her finest and that's no small compliment. I could tell that this trip meant as much to her as it meant to me. We sat for a moment and talked about her day, how she slept and what she watched on television. I told her I'd take her to the grocery store so she'd have snacks and drinks for the room because I wanted her to be as comfortable as possible. A few weeks before her trip she told me over the phone that she wanted to see me happy because she could tell I wasn't. Nicole asked me, "Is what you're doing today, going to get you where you want to be tomorrow?" Those words ran through my mind as I kept telling myself, "Date her today like you'll spend the rest of your lives together." For the first time in a long time I had my eyes on the future and the future began with one date, a second chance to show Nicole how seriously I took her and our relationship.

We left the hotel, drove to the restaurant and sat down for dinner. Nicole ordered Moscato like she did on our very first date and I ordered water. She and I both looked at one another and asked if we wanted to share a plate of calamari for an appetizer. We smiled and both said "yes." I remember on the first date telling Nicole that I had never been out with someone who ate calamari with me. I guess in love it really is the little things because that was 2008. It is 2015, we've been married for six years now, yet every-time we visit a new restaurant if they have it we try their calamari. It's become a tradition in our marriage that started back on our first date. We didn't know that awkward weekend in Ohio was the beginning of our lives together. We honestly didn't know much of anything back then. We were a young, hopeful couple with dreams. "Young, black, well educated and in love", was what we used to say to each other. We really thought we had the world at our fingertips. So on that night we sat, ate, drank, laughed and dreamed about what the future had in store for us. As we dined at the restaurant I started to re-evaluate my plans for the relationship I wanted with Nicole. I wanted the two of us to have a life that would be fulfilling not just for us personally but for us professionally as well. Nicole never struck me as the housewife type which was no problem for me because that wasn't the type of woman I wanted. I needed a partner that fit me. Nicole is an excellent writer, has an excellent sense of style and fashion, is photogenic, charming, entertaining and can sing her butt off. When I envisioned life with her I dreamed of us living our true passions and I wondered if those dreams would ever come true one day.

She and I finished dinner, stopped at the grocery store as planned to pick up some things for the room and then headed back to the hotel. We talked about our plans for the next day. I told her we could go somewhere I thought she'd like; my favorite local burger place. I think a part of me wanted to see if she would enjoy a $20 dinner as much as an expensive one but I already knew the answer was yes. She asked me what type of outfit she needed to wear for our night out on the town and I told her nothing too special, just something simple. That hotel room really was starting to feel like home. They say home is where the heart is and my heart was home wherever Nicole was. Life was starting to make sense. I always claimed I wanted a wife but before meeting Nicole I had no idea what a wife was. I thought a wife was someone pretty you got along with for life, maybe had some kids with in some big house in the suburbs and that was that until death did you part. A wife is so much more. A wife is a soul-mate, a help-mate, a friend and a partner. "He who finds a wife finds a good thing and receives favor from the Lord," is what the Bible says. In Nicole Singleton I had found a wife. We fell asleep peacefully that night and I arose and went to work the next morning. As soon as I got off I picked Nicole up and we went to shoot some pool and then afterwards sat and ate dinner at the burger joint. It was a nice night. I had the next two days off from work so we didn't stay out late that Wednesday because we knew we had a chance to spend some real time together over the next forty-eight hours. We returned to the hotel, watched television, ate and fell asleep again like an old married couple. Life honestly couldn't have felt any better.

That Thursday was a lazy day for us. Nicole had a long few days between graduation, traveling and hanging out with me, so we decided to spend the day laid up at the hotel. We found a show on television that caught our attention and spent several hours in bed. It was relaxing. We even got up later and went to grab some ice cream, then got some steak subs and went back to the hotel to crash. I told Nicole that on Friday I was taking her to the Lilac Festival in the park. The festival is a big event with vendors, artists and performers so I knew we'd be walking throughout the day and I didn't want to tire us out the night before. Friday, May 9th, 2009. We pulled up to the park and walked through the festival looking at the art, trying out the local food vendors and of course appreciating the beautiful flowers. I thought it'd be something different that she'd enjoy. We'd been out to dinner, we'd been to get ice cream, we'd had take out and went back to the room, so on Friday we spent the entire afternoon together. I got up first thing in the morning and went to cash my paycheck. I had a pocket full of money and was ready to spend it all on my lady. We walked through the park and had pecans and hot dogs. White hots, a Rochester, NY special. We ate, walked, talked and dreamed. I remember us getting lost in the neighborhood and walking past houses discussing whether or not we'd live there. What color houses we liked, what style, what type of driveway. Would we want flowers in our yard, a tree or both? We talked like an old couple walking down the street with nowhere to go. In that moment I knew I wanted Nicole to be my wife forever. I no longer had any doubts about it. I prayed for this woman and God answered my prayers. I felt like I had found my good thing. We eventually found our way out of the park and then went off to grab some dinner. We drove around looking for places to eat. Nicole spotted a restaurant neither of us had eaten at before so we decided we'd cap our night off with another first for the two of us. She and I have always tried to make the best out of the moments we share. Writing this book has been a much needed reflection for us. We "met" back in 2006, but didn't have our first visit together until two years and one long break-up later. That day at the Lilac festival was only the sixth day we'd ever spent together. We spent years talking and connected in some way or another but only six days physically together.

Shortly after Nicole had first arrived in Rochester she told me that her mother had given her the wedding ring that her father proposed to her with. Nicole knew I couldn't afford the kind of ring I wanted to get her but for months we'd been on the phone talking about whether we should get married or not. She told me if I didn't propose that we could be free to see other people. I clearly remember telling her that under no circumstances was her seeing other people cool with me. We talked about these things on the phone but I never proposed. She showed up to Rochester in the beginning of the week with an engagement ring for me to hand to her if I made up my mind about our future together. She told me when she gave me the ring, "Propose when you're ready." I went to bed on 5.9.08 thinking about Nicole. I had just gotten paid, and she had paid for most of our time together this visit. I had money now and I wanted to return the favor but Nicole knew I didn't make much. She knew I didn't have anything to 'blow,' on a good time. So when we woke up the next day, I asked her what she wanted to do and she told me, "I'm going home today, you work hard for your money, don't waste it." That was all the confirmation I needed and by that point I honestly shouldn't have needed anymore. We drove to my parents' house so she could drop me off. About five minutes before Nicole walked out of the door I pulled the ring she had given me out of my pocket and got down on one knee in my parents dining room. It was just the two of us. I told Nicole that I loved her. Told her she meant more to me than any woman in this world and then asked for her hand in marriage. To me it was a proposal; to Nicole it was simply a formality. Years later, she's quick to say we were engaged that entire trip and maybe we were, but I still had to make it official. I know some people would have felt weird about a man not being able to pay for his fiancé's ring but honestly I felt proud that her mother would even allow me to place such a keepsake on Nicole's finger. During our engagement I'd buy Nicole her own ring because her mother is a widow and deserved to have that memory of her husband, but the thought was truly an honor. I hugged her tightly before she got in her car. I gave her some money for gas and to get some food during her trip home; about $200 as we kissed and said goodbye. I sent her home with tears in my eyes. May 10th, 20008 was the day I asked Nicole Singleton to be Mrs. Richard Lawrence. On that day, my life changed forever.

***

Stand Your Ground (Nicole)

So, I know many of you are thinking "Nicole is crazy, why would she give Richard an ultimatum like that?" Fair question. My answer is simple. If you never express your expectations, you cannot expect a person to know how to treat you. It was obvious that in Richard's mind we were starting over after the year long hiatus. For me starting over was not even a possibility. Since Richard dictated the split and then came back asking forgiveness and a second chance, he needed to know I was open to letting him back into my life but the terms had changed. He had all say-so in the break up, I had say-so in the making up! I never deemed the marriage conversation as an ultimatum; I was simply putting all the options on the table, the choice was always his to make. I felt that I had already invested valuable time in the relationship why waste anymore just because it made him feel better when I wasn't comfortable with that? Sometimes in life we must decide to go-along-to-get-along, but your relationship is not one of those times. I made it very clear to Richard, either we're exclusive or we're both free to see other people but under no circumstance was I going to be put on pause waiting for him to grow decisive. Once you know what you're worth the list of things you're willing to accept gets extremely short and your tolerance for unhappiness even shorter.

Richard knew that I was unwilling to be a five to seven year girlfriend. We were not children anymore and if we knew we we're deeply in love why procrastinate? We were in love with each other, we both wanted to be married, most important we wanted to marry each other. What more did we have to wait on? Ladies, we have to stop letting the men make all the decisions in the relationship and then blame them for our unhappiness. Be real with yourself, if you don't speak up about your desires and step off in the event he doesn't step up, then you're a willing culprit in your own despondency. While it may be convenient to pass culpability to someone else, we as adults have to be able to take accountability in our lives. My advice is simple. Never settle on who you marry and abandon your expectations of love. However, you should never settle for love and give up your desire for marriage. You deserve both! When a person really wants you, nothing can keep them from you.

Work Today's Dream Until It's Tomorrow's Reality (Richard)

God placed you on this Earth and gave you a gift. The Lord placed inside of you a Gift and then placed someone else on this Earth to help you enlarge that gift into its intended purpose. People like to call that person their soul mate. However, the romantic perception of what a soul mate should be has overshadowed the divine distinction of what a soul mate is. Genesis 2:18 "The LORD God said, "It is not good for the man to be alone. I will make a helper suitable for him." Suitable for him. See, every man doesn't have the same gift, which means every man doesn't have the same purpose, every man doesn't require the same kind of help, but EVERY man requires help. It's not good for a man to be alone. I don't care what a lot of men say, they really don't know what to do with themselves by themselves, that's why he needs help, suitable help. So what's suitable help? While a man's physical needs may differ, his soul will always require a woman of character. Proverbs 31: 10-12 "A wife of noble character who can find? She is worth far more than rubies.11- Her husband has full confidence in her and lacks nothing of value. 12- She brings him good, not harm, all the days of her life."

People ask me all the time, "When did you know Nicole was the one?" About ten years ago, the night Nicole asked me what I wanted to be. And I told her what I thought I wanted to be at that time, and she responded, "Is what you're doing today going to get you where you want to be tomorrow?" I'd never had a woman take an interest in my future like that before, that was new to me. I wanted that connection, I needed that connection. See, I love that woman with all that's in me, but I realize that our love isn't enough. A man needs suitable help because it's not good for a man to be alone. A woman can't give a man purpose but she's heaven sent to help a man develop his gift into its intended purpose. Because it was written, 1Corinthians 7:7 "I wish that all men were as I am. But each man has his own gift from God; one has this gift, another has that." If you've found a woman to help you develop your gift into its God given purpose? You're truly blessed, I know I am!

CHAPTER SEVEN

Road Trip, No More...

I should have been mature enough to handle myself as a committed man earlier but I wasn't and I can fully admit that. Nicole left Rochester on May, 10th, 2008 with an engagement ring on her finger and she and I were finally getting married after years of off and on courtship. I was excited but knew that I had to officially end the relationships I had been carrying out with other women. When I re-entered Nicole's life back in November of 2007 I had been dealing with other women. I didn't consider myself seriously dating any of them but it didn't matter because I led them to believe we were in a serious relationship and for that I was wrong, but eight years ago you couldn't tell me I wasn't living life right. That's what they tell men, "Go out and play the field before you settle down." At whose expense? We never explain to our boys the true cost of playing with a woman's emotions. I wasn't honest in dating. I never believed a woman could accept a man if he told her honestly that he wasn't interested in a committed relationship. I was afraid of being honest and it affected my love life. Nicole and I were engaged but I hadn't told anyone other than my best-friend. I was scared to tell my parents because they hadn't met her and I didn't think they'd take our relationship seriously. She left on a Saturday and that same night I went out with my homeboy "Bread" to celebrate.

We went to a local bar and he bought me a couple of rounds. I told him I had gotten engaged to the girl I had talked to him about the past few months. We toasted and left the bar around 1am because Sunday was Mothers' Day. My mother had gone to Chicago to be with one of her sisters because she was ill while my father and I stayed in Rochester and planned to head to Brooklyn to visit my grandmother. My fathers' mom was the only grandparent I had left and she was in her early 90's, so I knew my time with her was precious and not to be taken for granted. I wanted her to be the first family member I told I was engaged. It was supposed to be a quick turn-around trip to Brooklyn. Six hours there, sit with Nana for Mother's Day, take her some flowers and head back upstate to Rochester. That was the plan but when Lawrence men are involved plans never matter. My father asked one of his friends to make the trip with us and we got on the road around 6am Sunday morning, a father and son headed to see the matriarch, you know the way "good men" are supposed to do.

It sounded nice except I woke up with a hangover because I'd been out drinking all night. My father and his friend had been out doing pretty much the same thing. So we have hung over men driving down the road headed to see the Queen of the Lawrence family and nobody's coming appropriately but at least we're coming right? WRONG! I made it about three-hundred miles down the road before I started nodding off at the wheel. I was fifty miles outside of Manhattan when I crashed into the guard rail doing 70 mph. The cop ran my license and comes back to the car to tell me it's suspended. I knew that already, so I'm prepared to go straight to jail. My dad tells the officer that he used to be a police officer too and promises him that he won't let me get behind the wheel again.

The police officer was very understanding and decided to let us go with a ticket and a shake of the head. I passed out in the backseat of the car until we finally made it to the nursing home where my grandmother lived. We sat around with Nana for about two hours. That woman had always meant the world to me. Summers with her and my great-aunts truly were some of the best memories I had in life. My Great aunts were gone, but I needed Nana to know about Nicole. As we got ready to leave the nursing home I told my father I needed to talk to my grandmother alone. He left the room and I sat in front of her, grabbed her hand and told her I had met a beautiful young lady named Nicole and we'd gotten engaged the day before. I told her that I thought she'd really like her and that she reminded me of her and my aunts. Nicole had an old school style to her that I loved from the moment I noticed it. I can tell that women like the ones who helped raise me helped to raise her and I knew that connection was a blessed one, so I wanted my grandmother to know that I had chosen a wife. Nana only asked me one question, "Are you happy?" I replied "yes ma'am" and then gave her a huge hug and said goodbye. As I walked to the elevator my fathers' friend asked what my Nana and I talked about. Before I could answer my father cut in and said, "Something we'll never know." If there's one thing Nana could do, it was keep a secret. I entrusted my grandmother with a secret I knew she'd keep. I hadn't told my parents I was engaged but I made sure to tell the oldest person alive on either side of the family. I was comfortable with that decision but I knew it would likely cause drama down the road. I didn't care though. I was engaged and my grandmother approved. It really doesn't get any better than that.

As my father, his friend and I headed home after one hell of a day, I was half passed out in the back seat texting Nicole telling her about my accident and letting her know I was alright. During the ride back upstate my father and his friend were discussing all the old men they used to hang out with. They thought I was asleep so they spoke freely. I'm listening to the two of them go down their list of friends name by name, calling off all the ones who had died before their time and as I was listening my father said something I'll never forget. He started talking about how all the men they knew who died before their time were a lot of the same men who ran out on their wives and families. He said, "Yeah see, all the ones who left their woman died early. Kids don't want anything to do with them, no family at the funeral. Mom buried him if she was still alive, if she wasn't he lucky if anybody buried him at all." I'm in the back seat listening to old men discuss how blessed they were to have women who loved them. Looking down at my phone I realized that I could have died that day and what that really meant. I called Nicole that night and we talked about how I was feeling. I told her that I was depressed. The last time we saw one another and the accident I had gotten into was wearing on me. I was really missing her. I needed her. The phone conversations weren't enough anymore. On those nights where I felt low, when I didn't have the strength to talk but needed to be near the woman I loved, the distance between us was a burden. I asked Nicole if she'd be willing to drive to New York for Memorial Day weekend. I didn't want to stay in Rochester, we'd done that. I visited Ohio once before to see her, but my time there was so short that we really didn't do anything other than go out to eat. I told Nicole if she was willing to make the trip to New York, I'd drive us back to Ohio for the weekend. Nicole agreed and we solidified our plans to spend the holiday together. She and I were engaged but we hadn't really discussed the elephant in the room; my family and how I hadn't told them about us. I'd met Nicole's mother on my first visit to Ohio but she didn't meet my parents on her first visit to New York and she wanted to know why? I battled back and forth for a long time about whether or not to tell my parents about her but I didn't exactly have the best relationship with them at the time. I love my parents, they'd do anything for me and they have supported me all the times I needed them, but that doesn't change the fact we haven't always had a pleasant relationship and as an adult I can finally own my part in that.

About a week before I first visited Nicole in February my parents and I had gotten into a huge argument. Police were called, no one was arrested but the officer did tell me that maybe I wanted to get myself together and leave because I was grown. It stings to hear that from a stranger, but I was feeling the same way. That was part of my problem at the time, I felt like a failure and had absolutely no idea or plan on how to succeed in life. I was frustrated and scared. I told Nicole about the two years in college I had spent living with my ex-girlfriend and how my parents objected to the situation because they felt like neither of us were ready for such a mature level of commitment. They were right of course but I learned after that relationship that it wasn't a good idea to involve your parents in your love life. Before meeting Nicole I had promised myself that I wouldn't introduce my family to a woman I was involved with until things were serious. Nicole and I were as serious as a couple could get. She still hadn't met my parents and I knew that needed to change and it would the weekend I left for Ohio in May of 2008. I remember the meeting well. Nicole arrived in Rochester around 2:30 Friday afternoon. My father wasn't home, but my mother was. I knew the questions would come flying the moment my mother saw her, because Nicole was wearing her engagement ring and my mother wasn't aware that I was engaged.

My mother and Nicole stood in the kitchen exchanging pleasantries that honestly weren't so pleasant. You could sense the tension and awkwardness in the room but I knew that butting into the conversation would only undermine my fiancé. She was more than capable of standing her ground with anyone. My mother asked Nicole what college she attended, what her degree was in, what she planned on using that degree for and where she had worked in the past? The questions didn't end there. She asked her how many siblings she had. Nicole responded that she had an older brother. She asked if Nicole's parents were married. Nicole responded yes they were for over twenty years, until death did them part and left her mother widowed. The intrusive questions kept coming and all I could do was watch as Nicole answered each and every question like a seasoned interview candidate because it truly felt as though she was being interviewed for the position of my significant other. The questions finally came to an end as I gathered up my luggage and packed Nicole's car preparing for the return trip to Ohio. I let Nicole know I was finished and that we could leave whenever she was ready. She said goodbye to my mother, and the two of us headed back to Ohio to spend the holiday together.

While in the car we talked about how Nicole felt meeting my mother for the first time. She told me she felt uncomfortable. She felt as though my mother asked questions that implied she wasn't, "good enough," for me and it was tactless. I asked Nicole was she upset that I didn't stand up for her and she said no because she knew that I couldn't. She knew she had to speak for herself to be respected by my mother. Deep down I think every man wants his wife and mother to get along but it honestly didn't seem like my wife and mother were destined for that type of relationship. Nicole and I went on to enjoy our weekend. I honestly don't remember much of what we did during my time in Ohio that trip except for one night out with some friends of hers. A married couple she was friends with invited us out to dinner. Nicole and I sat down, ate, drank and enjoyed a wonderful meal with them. What made the evening memorable for me was when the waiter came to the table with our check. Nicole and I had spent around eighty dollars on our meal that night. As I reached into my pocket to pull out some money to pay for dinner, Nicole grabbed my hand and slid me her debit card under the table. Then she quietly leaned over, gave me a kiss and whispered, "Save your money." I remember placing Nicole's card for the waiter to pick up, and smiling to myself and thinking, "If my mother only knew just how qualified to be my wife she was." She is not the type of woman who feels empowered by demeaning a man. She doesn't aggressively and annoyingly display her ability to be an independent woman. She just is, effortlessly! No matter the situation she never treats me like anything less than a man.

Up until that weekend, Nicole and I weren't sure whether or not we'd live in New York, or in Ohio. I had the more stable job in New York and she had the more welcoming family situation for us in Ohio. We made our way back to Rochester as the weekend drew to a close. This was the third visit Nicole and I had spent together and it was genuinely becoming harder and harder to say goodbye. I made up in my mind that I didn't want Nicole to move to New York. I was certain I would have better luck finding a job in Ohio than she would finding one in Rochester. I had been out of school longer, had the more established resume and was willing to take whatever job was necessary to get off my feet. Honestly, after watching the meeting between Nicole and my mother I knew that living in Rochester would only cause a strain on our impending marriage. It was clear to me at the time that my mother didn't approve and that was a battle I didn't want to fight. My mind was all over the place on that drive back home as Nicole and I talked.

We arrived in Rochester late Sunday evening around 11pm. She was going to turn right back around and drive to Ohio but I couldn't let the woman I love drive all night. I was worried about her safety. Then I remembered her sliding me her debit card at the restaurant during the trip. She was trying to save me some money because she knew I didn't have much and she didn't want to see me spend my last dime on her. I asked her if she'd be willing to spend the evening in NY and get some rest then drop me at work in the morning. Nicole agreed and we spent that evening together at a hotel lying in bed watching television. We didn't even make love that night. I think we were too tired and in love to make love. We held one another, kissed and passed out in each other's arms. The next morning she dropped me off at work. I remember getting out of the car and hugging her in the street as school was about to start. A few children walked past and saw us embracing. I kissed Nicole and with tears in my eyes wished her safe travels. I've never experienced a goodbye as hard as that one. I wiped my face and prepared myself to walk into the building. I had spent so much time over the years shedding tears of sadness. For once I was shedding tears because I was truly happy and Nicole's love made me realize there was more worth living for. That Monday morning as she got in her car and headed back to Ohio is the day I knew I never wanted to say goodbye to Nicole again not knowing when the next time we'd see each other would be. Something had to give.

***

Staying Steadfast (Nicole)

Meeting Richard's mother for the first time was uncomfortable to say the least. It wasn't that I never anticipated questions upon our first encounter; I just presumed the questions would be a little more general the first meeting. In all honesty the entire incident felt less like an inquisitive or concerned mother and more like a detective playing the role of "good cop." Her tone gave me complete insight to what I was dealing with. The questions she asked let me know that she was experienced in the art of "nasty-nice." An art women have utilized for centuries. I guess it is just one of our catty attributes. You do know what nasty nice is right? It is when a person speaks in a seemingly pleasant tone yet the actual words are full of insinuation and venom. I was cool, calm and collected on the exterior but internally I was fuming. I mean seriously, how dare she attempt to look down on me? What did she have to gain attempting to make me wither with self doubt? To add insult to injury it was clear she didn't deem me bright enough to notice exactly what she was attempting to do. I felt totally disrespected. Why not just observe my mannerisms and then privately make an assessment of me and my lineage? I pride myself on being intelligent, poised, classy, witty, respectful and respectable. She didn't know then but I knew she would learn eventually because I was going to be around for the long haul. I refused to let my age or lack of experience allow her to presume I would succumb to the pressure. I remained polite, poised and matter-of-factly.

While I was temporarily bothered I knew there was a bigger picture. Richard and I were in love and his mother's not so discreet disapproval couldn't change that. It was in that moment that I gained greater insight to what Richard had been trying to express to me. His hesitation in revealing our engagement began to make sense. It was also in that moment that I decided to avoid ever being a negative energy in his life. I love him! Love is not abrasive or mean. Love is not overcritical or judgmental. Love is not cruel, bossy, or manipulative. We were finally moving past personal hurdles and there was no way I was going to let anything stand in the way of our love, not even his mother's disapproval.

If ever you're faced with a similar issue, remain steadfast in who you are. Be strong in your convictions and never allow another individual to knock you of your square. Keep your character in tact because it's who you truly are that matters most, people's perception of you is not your concern. Express yourself but always maintain your wits about yourself, because eventually the other person(s) will lose their cool and you'll be left looking like the sane one!

Dealing With Outside Influences (Richard)

Outside influences can be a strain on a couple's relationship if they allow others to intrude on their love. Dealing with outsiders is a life-long task everyone has to face. I believe there are three things a couple can do to protect the privacy of their union.

3 Tips To Protect Your Union's Privacy

1.) A couple should always support one another in front of family and friends: There will be times when you'll find it hard to support your partner in public. For example, they may say something wrong, may do something wrong and your embarrassment and/or love will want to correct them. Be mindful of how you do so. Can the correction be done discretely? Can your opinion be offered without making the one you love look bad? Should you wait for a better time to let your partner know their mistake? Be mindful of how you interact with your partner in front of others and attempt to do so in a way that makes your loved one feel supported and never chastised. A united front is integral.

2.) A couple should try not to argue in public: Arguing in public is always an awkward and unsettling moment both for the couple and those around. It casts an unpleasant image over your union. People wonder, "If they behave like this in front of us, what do they do in private?" Arguing with your mate is natural, all couples endure disagreements but in public it's unhealthy. Agree to disagree and revisit the issue later when you have privacy.

3.) Do not allow the doubts others have about your relationship or partner negatively impact your union: When friends and family make negative remarks about your mate and/or relationship they are hard to ignore and often they eventually begin to seep in if you allow them to. For example, your mother says that your husband isn't a good provider, and then he loses his job and you begin to say the same. Your friends say your wife nags too much, and now every time she asks you to do something you feel like she won't get off your back. It's hard to tune out the influences of others when they're constantly around. Love your family and friends but if they're constantly belittling your mate or union, limit your exposure to the negativity before it begins to influence your relationship in an unhealthy manner.

CHAPTER EIGHT

Uprooting

Life is funny! I had messed around and fallen in love under the most unlikely circumstances with a woman I couldn't stand to spend a day without. Life didn't feel right without her. I didn't feel fulfilled when she wasn't near. She had become a part of me and I truly felt as though we were becoming one.

I was battling a big decision. I knew I was leaving Rochester but when and how were the questions. I knew I would have to resign from a job I had just recently been hired full time at and that I would be giving up money, life insurance, health insurance; all those things a married man needs to provide for his wife and family. I was scared of what people would say. I knew whatever decision I made would likely be deemed the wrong one but I had to do what was right for me. Being with Nicole was right for me. Our last visit together affected me differently. Since returning home we'd talk all afternoon about our day, her job search, my job search, our impending move, and the upcoming wedding. Nicole had already begun making plans and purchasing small trinkets we'd need for our wedding day. She purchased wedding invitations and wine glasses for the head table; baby-girl was dutifully going about setting our nuptials in stone. September 5[th,] 2009 was to be the fateful day, the day before Nicole's 25th birthday. I was excited but becoming more and more worried about what I thought the future would hold. I had been actively looking for a job in Ohio for months but hadn't received any call backs and was becoming frustrated. I was certain that if I was unable to find employment it would weigh heavy on our relationship somewhere down the line. A man is supposed to provide, that's what everyone says. I was unsure of my ability to provide for the woman I loved. I was uncertain of my ability to be a man worthy of her hand in marriage.

I was scared. I was a twenty-five year old engaged man with nothing to call my own. Nothing to give the woman I loved but a smile and my heart. Not exactly a welcoming package and I knew that. I was feeling like a failure. I had no one to talk to about what I was going through and felt like I couldn't tell Nicole because I couldn't see her loving me if she knew how messed up I really was. As if my flaws were something that could be hidden. I guess at the time I thought they were. I kept telling myself I was intelligent, kind, hard-working and dedicated to family when the truth was I was lazy, unmotivated and only cared about myself. Nicole was never fooled; she never lied to herself about who I was. I realized that one night on the phone right before June rolled in. The school year was almost over and she and I were discussing whether I would come spend the summer in Ohio and look for a job once I was there. It wasn't long before the discussion about me coming to Ohio turned into Nicole and me talking about her first time meeting my mother. The experience was very uncomfortable for her.

Nicole felt as if my mother was interrogating her to see if she had the "pedigree" to be with me. Insinuating she wasn't good enough to date me. She began asking about my relationship with my parents. I told her that I was truly feeling depressed about my living situation. I wanted to move but couldn't afford to. I told Nicole I felt stuck. I told her I was terrified I wouldn't be able to provide for her. I wanted to take care of her but didn't feel like I could. I worried that one day she'd realize she fell in love with a loser and move on to someone new. If I were her that's probably what I would have done. I used to tell Nicole all the time that I knew she could do better than me. I'll never forget what she said that night: "I don't need you to take care of me Richard; I'm more than capable of taking care of myself. I never asked you to provide for me, I asked you to love me, to be faithful to me, to respect me, to work your hardest, try your best and always be honest. That's all I need from you. We can make the rest happen together. If you move here I got you, I got us. Provide for me what you can initially and NEVER stop striving to provide for us to the greatest of your abilities. That's all I can ask." I asked her if she was sure because it sounded almost too good to be true. I didn't want to believe her. I felt like no woman would really hold true to such a bold promise. All I could think about was the years my father was unemployed when I was younger and all the dysfunction it caused for my parents. The arguments, the bills piling up, the stress; the combination of it all was very overwhelming. As a child I never cared because my dad was always there for me during those years. He cooked for me, he helped me with my homework, he walked me to school in multiple feet of snow as I sat on his shoulders; what child wouldn't cherish those moments? He was never anything less than a man to me. Those years may have been incredibly taxing for my parents but they were priceless to me.

I wondered if Nicole and I were strong enough to survive that kind of difficulty. We'd already dealt with my unwillingness to commit. We dealt with me walking out on her when she needed a friend most. I'd already abandoned her once and I felt like not being able to provide would be abandonment yet again. I finally broke down and told her all of that and for the first time in my life I felt like I was talking to someone who cared. Nicole told me she could sense the pressure I was feeling from home to be successful in a career that wasn't my passion and encouraged me to give up that "dream" and discover my own, months earlier. But on this night she was encouraging me to go a step further; she told me she thought it'd be best if I moved to Ohio. The suggestion caught me off guard.

We'd talked about me possibly moving to Ohio or her to New York but neither of us committed to moving either place until that night on the phone in early June. I told Nicole she didn't have to do that, I wasn't asking or expecting her to essentially take me in. That's never what I wanted. She quickly told me, "This may not be what you want, but moving here and getting out of your parents home is what you need. I really believe you need to get out of that environment; it's not healthy for you. I don't doubt they were amazing parents, I fell in love with the man they raised, but you're a man and you have to live the life you want or you'll suffocate and end up resentful." She was right. We talked on and on that evening, never coming to any real resolution, but at least we were finally talking about our future. I began making plans to spend my summer in Ohio but like people have always told me if you want to make God laugh tell the Lord what you have planned.

They proved to be very precise as far as my life was concerned. I was at work one day when I was called into the Principals' office. A parent had come to school to issue a complaint about the way she felt I treated her son. As I sat in the office and listened to this parent essentially tell me all the reasons she felt I shouldn't teach, all I could think in my head was, "This is not the career for me."If I needed a sign that it was time to move on, that was surely it. The complaint was nothing major that would have cost me my job, I was fully supported by my supervisors and co-workers and for that I was very thankful but I realized that I did not have what it took to spend my life teaching. That was not the field for me. After meeting with the parent I went to the computer lab and began typing my official letter of resignation from the Rochester City School District. I went down to the office to make leaving work official. The head secretary could tell I was upset by the events that took place earlier in the day. She was normally mean to people when they came into the office but on that day she was the sweetest person anyone could have been to me. I had worked at that school off and on for almost four years and my co-workers had grown to respect me. The secretary looked over the time I had available to take off for the school year and informed me that she'd make sure I'd be paid for the last two weeks of school. She covered me with the rest of my vacation and sick days and wished me well as I left the building. I walked out of work that day, Thursday June, 12th, 2008, no longer a teacher's aide, no longer employed. My first phone call was to Nicole. I told her everything that had just happened, how the parent had come up to the school and how I had submitted my letter of resignation. Nicole seemed shocked but honestly not surprised and a decision was made. I asked Nicole if it would be possible for her to come get me.

Nicole told me she needed a few hours to move some things around but she could be in New York by 9am the next morning which worked out great for me. I had been planning to throw a pizza party for my basketball team. I also wanted to say a final goodbye to some of my co-workers who'd been so supportive. Nicole arrived in NY as planned around 9:30am on Friday. My parents were out of town that week. I knew that when they came home and realized I had quit both my job and school they wouldn't be happy with me, particularly my mother. The agreement we had was as long as I was working and in school, I could live at home rent free without paying any bills. I was no longer working or in school, and I knew the reality of that would make for a hard time at home. I realized that at twenty-five I should have been able to make my own decisions free from worrying what anyone else may have to say but that wasn't the case. I was very worried about how my parents would react to the news of what had taken place the past several days. I was burned out. It was affecting me negatively and I needed to go. It was time to move on. I honestly had no idea what I was moving on to as far as a career, but as far as life, I was ready to begin a new one with Nicole. The life I was living wasn't happy and to drag her into my unhappiness just because it offered immediate security wouldn't have been fair. Nicole and I deserved a fresh start and we couldn't do that while I was tied down to an old life that was never for me.

Nicole was understandably tired from driving all night long. I left her at my parents' house while I ran some errands preparing for our trip back to Ohio. I went to the post office to forward my mail, went to the bank, got a haircut and then picked up pizzas for the party with the children at work. I went back to my parents' house to get her so she could attend the party with me. It had been a long day, and I wanted to get her home. We packed up her car with my belongings and headed to the school so I could give my basketball team their end of the year celebration, say goodbye to the children and farewell to my co-workers. Before leaving my mom and dad's, I wrote a note on a piece of paper letting them know I had left to go to Ohio along with my cell phone number. Months earlier after a heated argument I told my mother I was moving to Ohio and for weeks she mocked me about it as if I was playing. Nicole asked me if I was going to call her and let her know I was leaving for good, but I told Nicole it would only start drama we didn't need. Looking back, it would have been the right thing to do and I should have done it but I can honestly say I didn't have the strength to deal with the situation at that moment. For the first time in a very long time I was happy. I called Nicole frantically to come get me and less than twelve hours later she was at my front door. Never in my life had I experienced a love like that and I was ecstatic about what the future would hold for the two of us. She had helped me to find peace in my life. I had never really understood what being at peace felt like because I was never comfortable enough to sit still. I was never comfortable enough alone to truly enjoy being alone and I learned that wasn't healthy. My lack of self love prevented me from truly giving love. Falling in love with Nicole meant nights at home alone on the phone with her and having to be happy with that because at one point it was all we had. For a long time it never felt like enough because I didn't love myself enough to appreciate it.

Nothing about the move was planned or well thought out and only time would tell whether Nicole and I would pay for my impulsiveness. I'm sure many people would say I was making a horrible decision but my life changed dramatically over the course of forty-eight hours. The truth is the process began when I saw Nicole Singleton online two years earlier. Then we stopped talking and I wondered if I'd ever speak to her again? We re-connected and then I wondered if we were meant to be together? Now here we were engaged and after everything we had endured she and I were finally on our way home to start our lives together. The one thing we never questioned was approaching what was next together. I'd lost my job and messed around and found my good thing. Life's funny!

* * *

When Love Calls (Nicole)

When Richard called me frantic and clearly overwhelmed, there was no question I was going to assist in whatever way I could. When he said he was ready to suddenly give up everything and move to Ohio, I'll admit I was excited he wanted to move to Ohio but it seemed irrational. He was just stressed; I mean was he really ready to leave everything familiar for a new and foreign existence without a blueprint? My intent was to hop in the car and make the trip regardless, just to give him some time to think. I missed him dreadfully so it would be great to be with him, even if it turned out to be nothing more than just another visit. Richard was full of emotion when he called and I knew he just needed a listening ear. I knew that wasn't the right moment to utter sensibility to him. I needed to allot him the time to live in that emotion. Often we want to offer up advice versus allowing our loved one to momentarily dwell in the emotion. Give them the opportunity to come to some resolve on their own before offering unsolicited advice. When your loved one reaches out to you it's because they want to talk, don't deprive them of that. We perceive it as being helpful when giving advice, sometimes the most helpful thing we can do is simply be a sounding board, only there to listen. He wanted to escape and I was going to be that escape for him. While I knew the leap to moving with no security was irrational and irresponsible that was not the time to express those feelings. Honestly, what harm could my support in his wanting to leave town do? He would either 1.) get there, clear his mind and enjoy some quality time with his fiancé before deciding to go back to New York and work it out or 2.) decide that he made the right decision and remain in Ohio to start a new more fulfilling life. Either way, he was bound to find some source of happiness and he deserved that!

When your lover calls out to you never be too busy to answer. You don't have to place undue pressure on yourself by attempting to fix everything. Simply listen and be supportive. Love is frequently quiet and in that silence so many answers can be found. Just be there. If they need advice they'll ask so until then just be a loving support system.

Listen With Love (Richard)

One of the hardest things to do as a mate is to not try and fix your partners problems when they come to you with issues that are worrisome. It is human nature to want to help the ones we love feel better and often we try to solve their problems without really allowing them a chance to vent. Listening to your partner with love is one of the most caring things you can do to show support for your mate. Some tips on how to listen with love.

3 Tips To Listen Lovingly

1.) **Give your mate your undivided attention**: When your loved one comes to you with an issue do your best to be fully involved. Put down your cell-phone, turn off the television and try to limit any distractions that'd give your mate the impression you're not really listening or vested in their problem. A major part of listening with love is giving your mate your full attention in order to let them know their problem is important not only to them, but to you as well.

2.) **Be respectful**: When listening to your mate express themselves there may come a time when they say something you do not like and/or disagree with. Express your disagreement respectfully. Many times we forget to be polite with the one we love because we take for granted that they know what we "really" meant when we said something. A polite, "Dear, I think you may be wrong," or a soft-spoken "Honey, I disagree with you," goes a long way towards keeping a partnership happy. When listening to your partner always remember to be respectful in your response. Being respectful is an example of your love.

3.) **Don't make the conversation about you:** Your mate tells you something bad happened to them like they've just lost their job, and before they tell you how it makes them feel, you interject, "What will WE do?" Inserting yourself into your partner's problem before they've asked for your opinion often makes people feel like what they're dealing with is secondary or altogether unimportant. Give your spouse the freedom to express themselves without making the conversation about you.

CHAPTER NINE

Destination Unknown

It is said everything happens for a reason. That ride from Rochester to Columbus was a somber one for me. I was excited on one end but scared on the other. Nicole and I weren't ready. We weren't prepared for what life had in store and I knew it. We were in our twenties, impulsive, filled with hopes and dreams of a happy marriage, family and successful careers. Like many couples our dreams exceeded our realities and that's dangerous. A couple should be grounded in reality, but Nicole and I were dreaming because like baby girl always says, "Sometimes you got to fake it until you make it." We were well on our way to faking stability. She and I talked about what we both knew was coming on that long trip home, my mothers' reaction to me leaving Rochester and quitting my job. We both knew it wouldn't be positive, so we debated back and forth about when we'd decide to tell my parents about our engagement.

Nicole's friends and family already knew, only two people in my life knew and I knew that would have to change sooner than later. She and I hadn't talked about our potential wedding party, and I knew I wanted relatives to be in our wedding but I also knew that would take plenty of planning because of location. None of my family lived in Ohio and most of my family didn't live in New York either, so no matter where I got married a vast majority of them would have to travel, which means I'd have to tell them early that I was getting married if I expected them to come. There was no way I could tell anyone on either side of my family and not expect my mother to find out eventually. Honestly, Nicole and I both figured she knew anyway because Nicole never took her engagement ring off when they met, but we also never made it official in her presence. We arrived in Ohio and headed to her mother's apartment. Nicole had returned home the semester before she graduated from college and was planning on moving out again but now Nicole and I were living with her mother. I honestly didn't know what to expect but I trusted my wife and that trust carried me through the feelings of uncertainty.

One of the reasons I fell in love with Nicole was hearing her speak so lovingly about her father. Never was her love for her father rooted in how much money he made, how many bills he paid, the car he drove or anything materialistic. She admired her father's hard work, heart and dedication to his family. She admired how hard he tried when a lot of other men would have quit. She admired how her mother made a larger more stable salary than her father but never used that to make him feel less of a man. I appreciated that Nicole valued her father because he never quit, even when layoffs and strikes occasionally forced him out of work. She always told me that I can only fail if I don't try. The first time she told me that I realized that I was failing at life because I hadn't tried yet. I hadn't really tried because I hadn't found my purpose. I was determined to try and make this move work and the encouragement she offered was my security blanket. I started to believe in myself and us.

Once upon a time I prayed to God for Nicole and told him that if he delivered that gift to me, I'd do whatever he wanted me to do. As I sit here writing about the representation of God's first union, it dawns on me that you better be careful what you pray for, you just might get it. All I ever wanted to do was write a book about MY family. Before Nicole all I could do was tell my mother and father's story. My Grandparents story but I couldn't tell my own story, because I didn't have one worth reading. When I kept looking for confirmation of my purpose she refused to give it. She refused to tell me what to do with my life because it wasn't her place to direct my path. She didn't want me to resent her for a decision she never should have had to make. So when I started writing about us, when I started talking about our relationship, lives, love and marriage Nicole never told me to stop. When I was up all night writing, she never said come to bed. She watched, supported and probably thanked God her husband finally found his purpose, and for that I'm thankful.

All I knew when I stepped inside of her mothers' apartment in June was that I was in Ohio now, living with my fiancé and my future mother-in-law, unemployed with no prospect of a job. Not the most comfortable position for a man to be in. The first several weeks were great. We went out to eat regularly, played pool, hung out all day, spent time with her friends; there was nothing for us to complain about. Then around mid July my paychecks from work stopped coming in. I had two paychecks from work forwarded to me throughout the month of July because my job was on a time delay. The money ran out and the arguments soon followed. I had tried my best to show Nicole and her mother I wasn't there to use them. The last thing I wanted was for them to think I was some no good man who just wanted to lounge around their house and live off of them. All I heard in my head was them sitting around saying, "This man isn't worth a damn." That's all I was telling myself and Nicole paid the price for my lack of confidence.

The worst argument came one Saturday afternoon. Nicole was going to one of her friend's house for a ladies night. We had been fussing for days and honestly needed some time apart. She left home around six in the evening and I sat around watching television and playing on the computer. Hours started to go by and I began to worry. We had hung out over Nicole's friend's house many times by that point, so I figured she'd be home around 11pm, midnight at the latest. I was wrong because she and her girls decided they wanted to go out to the bar to grab some drinks. I called her around 1 am and she told me that she was in the club hanging out. She didn't drive and was waiting for her friends to leave so she could return home.

It would be almost 4am when she returned home and the second she walked through the door we went at it. Yelling and hollering loud enough to wake up the neighbors. Nicole's crying, I'm threatening to leave and go home, all because of a lack of communication on both of our parts. Now we were arguing with each other and threatening to end our relationship less than two months after it really began. I've learned one of the most hurtful things anyone can do in a relationship is threaten to leave in a moment of anger, but at that time I hadn't come to that point in my life. I was bitter about my circumstances and felt like I had every reason to take it out on Nicole. In my mind she was out all night looking for another man. I just knew she was tired of supporting me, what woman wouldn't be? I kept telling myself she could do better and I was scared she was feeling the same way. My insecurity was eating away at my ability to love her.

Nicole and I would go inside the house and make our way to sleep that night, but it wasn't a happy sleep. We didn't sleep in the same bed together because we were both so angry and the argument spilled into the next day. I was walking around upset trying to make her pay for the way I felt the night before. I wanted her to hurt the same way I hurt when all she wanted to do was love me and apologize. She'd made an honest mistake. She never intended to be out that late and wasn't doing anything wrong but I wasn't ready to receive what she was saying because I was too bitter to believe her. After hearing us argue throughout the morning, Nicole's mother came to talk to me about what had gone on the night before. I just knew, this was it. I totally expected her mother to ask me to leave their home. What she did, I wasn't prepared for but I thank God for it till this very day. Nicole's mother sat down and said, "I know why you're upset. You're trying real hard and things haven't broken for you yet, but it is ok we all go through hardships sometimes. You're trying and that's all you can do. Nobody's looking at you like you aren't trying your hardest and you're welcome here. This is your home."

I'll never forget those words. In that moment, after arguing with my fiancé and feeling as though I had failed her, her mothers' encouragement helped to keep me strong and by extension kept Nicole and I strong as well. Relationships have to deal regularly with external forces, both positive and negative ones. In a moment of uncertainty and frustration Nicole's mother had become a positive influence on us but she was not the only influence we had to contend with. Nicole knew that if we were going to tell my parents we were engaged they had to believe we could support ourselves or we'd never hear the end of it. Not that their opinion should have ever mattered but Nicole knew it mattered greatly to me and impacted the both of us because of that. About a week after Nicole and I argued over her being out all night and my mishandling of the discussion, my parents called me with news. They were vacationing down south and were planning on stopping in Ohio for a few hours to see how Nicole and I were doing before they headed home to NY. We knew that really they were coming to check up on our living situation, and Nicole went to work in a way I've come to admire about her. She made sure I looked good. A good wife takes great measure to make sure her husband always looks good, and I was going to be Nicole's husband so she made sure I looked good at all times if she had anything to say about it. On my parents' first visit to Ohio, she had everything to say about it. My parents were traveling with my Aunt Theresa and Uncle Aaron. They didn't plan to stay long, just long enough to eat, say hello and be nosy.

She and I got busy cooking and cleaning the apartment in preparation for their visit. Nicole's mother planned to be away while my parents were there. She had gone to her sisters' house and told us to call her once my parents left. Nicole told her mother that my parents did not need to know we lived with her. They wouldn't approve. That first visit was pleasant, but you could easily feel the tension in the atmosphere. Nicole didn't wear her engagement ring, but only because relatives were with my parents and we didn't want the entire family to know until we could tell them ourselves on our own terms. The entire time my parents were there it felt like my mother was looking for reasons why Nicole and I being together was a bad decision. We didn't feel supported, not that we expected her support. The visit was over briefly and my family got on the road headed home. That visit was the first time Nicole had met my father. The visit itself seemed like a nice one but I told Nicole to expect drama to follow it. There were trivial questions asked while they were there like, "Where are you working? Do you plan on coming home?" Just the normal intrusive questions any mother asks when trying to figure out all of their child's business.

Nicole and I made a very conscious decision to protect our privacy. We were learning early on in our relationship that privacy is necessary. I hated keeping the details of our relationship a secret but I truly felt like the longer my parents didn't know the better off Nicole and I would be during our engagement. We talked and we decided we'd tell my parents about our wedding plans in December of 2008. Our wedding was scheduled for September 5th, 2009, so that still gave my family a full nine months to prepare and Nicole and I several months to make plans without dealing with drama we couldn't control. After my parents left we went out to a friends' house. We sat up playing spades, drinking and talking about the wedding and who would be in the wedding party. Nicole told her friend she'd be Matron of honor and then Nicole asked me who'd be my best man? I told her my homeboy Bread more than likely because he'd been a best man before and I trusted he could get the job done. Then I asked Nicole if she'd be willing to let two of my cousins be bridesmaids. My cousins Erica and Latoya were like little sisters to me and I really wanted them to be included. Nicole agreed, which said a lot about the type of woman she was because she hadn't met either lady yet but she'd heard me talk about them both and knew they were close to me so she embraced them with open arms. The next day I called Erica and told her I was engaged then gave her my number to have Latoya call me so I could tell her the same. They both agreed to be in the wedding, and for the first time since being in Ohio I was happy. I felt supported.

The reaction of my cousins hearing about me getting married to a woman they hadn't even had the pleasure of meeting reminded me that my family was bigger than just my mother. In my rush to invite my cousins to be a part of our wedding I failed to take into account the unintended consequences. I told both of my cousins to keep our engagement a secret because I hadn't told my parent's yet and they agreed but we all know how family and secrets go. Nicole asked me, "How long do you think it'll be before your parents find out we're engaged?" I had no answer, but for the moment I was excited and didn't care. Nicole and I were beginning to lay down serious wedding plans. By the time August rolled around she had found a new job. I continued looking for work with no success but was determined not to give up. Nicole began saving up for us to move out into our own place. August turned into September when I received some mail one day from my old job. My former supervisor had never turned in my letter of resignation and the school district was writing to inform me that I had thirty days to return to work or forfeit my position. I showed the letter to Nicole and told her, "Baby, I've never been unemployed, I've always had a job and didn't realize it, do you want me to go back home and send you money to prepare for the wedding?" Nicole said to me, "Do what you want, whatever makes you happy, but I don't need you to go home and send me money, we'll be alright."

Those words burned deep into my soul. Her reassurance was everything I needed at the time, especially when I had every reason to doubt myself. I still wasn't sure of what the future held, but I typed a new letter of resignation and continued my search for a new job in Ohio. A month after I resigned for good, I started work at the same place Nicole had found a job two months earlier. It wasn't my dream job, but it was a start and I was making more money than I'd ever made before so things began to look up. We were both employed, saving and preparing to move out on our own. Progress was coming slow but it was coming. All that was left to do was announce our engagement and jumping that broom. Like many couples our dreams exceeded our realities and that's dangerous. A couple must be grounded in reality, but Nicole and I were dreaming because like baby girl always says, "Sometimes you got to fake it till you make it." It finally started to seem like we were finally making it through the drama, Lord knows we needed reasons to smile again. I was tired of faking it but with everything she and I had been through I was just grateful we were making our own way. What doesn't kill you makes you stronger, so I guess it's true what they say, everything happens for a reason. In so many ways our strength as a couple was being tested, but with every trial we faced our dedication, commitment and love for each other grew stronger.

***

Understanding The Unsaid (Nicole)

When we had our first argument it was hard but it was necessary. I mean come on, fairy tales aren't real and we were going to have to face that reality eventually. That argument made me realize that adjusting from single/dating life to married life was not going to come automatically. Lesson learned. During the early stages of our relationship hardships took no mercy upon us; adjustments, unemployment, under-employment, financial woes, intrusive and disrespectful outsiders and living together proved to be much more than either of us bargained for. Growing up witnessing my parent's marriage I never truly considered the possible complexities of a marriage or in our case a pending marriage. That in itself is a blessing; I was a child and deserved nothing less than an innocent childhood as does every child. My parents kept their adult marital issues to themselves. Underneath occasional struggle there shined love still stronger than ever so quitting was never a consideration. I was learning that one of the biggest relationship tribulations was people other than ourselves. Our love life was actually awesome; it was every other aspect that we struggled with. That's the funny thing about life; you cannot have the good without the bad. I was so pleased that Richard was able to find solace in knowing that he did have his extended family's support. All I cared about was his happiness and sanity. I know it sounds mean; maybe even cynical but the fact that I wasn't a favorite to his mother was less than irrelevant to me. My thought process was straight-forward, I had a supportive family, he had supportive family members, we had God and each other. If all of that wasn't comfort enough there was a 400 mile distance, highways and state borders between his mother and us. The disdain and disapproval couldn't affect my daily life, I decided it wasn't allowed. My concern was remaining the child of God I was, the woman my mother taught me to be, and becoming the wife Richard both needed and deserved!

I know our relationship breakdown was simply Richard lashing out emotionally. We had a ton of stress, anyone would break down. I decided it was not going to be me. He needed me to stay strong although he never said so but the truth is I knew I was strong enough to be his rock. Sometimes love requires you to understand the unsaid. I am not saying be a mind reader just be observant. Know your spouse. Know that they need your support, your strength and most importantly your love before they ever have to ask for it. It is not rocket science, just be attentive and realize that in a relationship there will be give and take. There will be times where you're not afforded the opportunity to be vulnerable because it is not your turn. Richard and I excel at supporting each other during the other's time of need. We've observed what areas of distress the other displays as a breaking point so we step in and pick up the pieces for each other. A marriage will not survive hardships if both parties checkout. A car with an irrational driver or no driver at all is sure to crash and burn. If the destination is "until death does us part", someone must always be at the wheel.

Give And Take (Richard)

A relationship thrives on give and take. In a loving union when one partner falls down the other rises up and leads until their mate regains their composure and strength. Reciprocity is the basis of love. There have been times in our relationship where I was unable to lead and in those moments needed support and guidance in order to rise to the occasion. Nicole always gave me that support, but instead of giving her the same I just took and our relationship suffered because of it.

Men and women have different needs but what will always be the same among us is our need to be loved. We all need to be loved in our own way. Whether men can admit it or not they like to feel rewarded for their hard work. Talk to a man and he'll tell you about what he needs. He needs sex, he needs a good meal, he needs peace, he needs to feel appreciated for the things he provides. Those bills he pays, that love he shows. Women aren't any different. If she's been supportive, tender and nurturing the last thing she wants to deal with is a man she can't trust. If a man's been providing for a woman he feels is unappreciative he grows distant. When a woman can't trust a man to provide for her in ALL the ways she needs she finds it hard to love a man the way he requires. A man and a woman may show love differently but for a relationship to work love MUST always be given, received & reciprocated.

I knew what I needed from Nicole but never took time to ask her what she needed from me and for that I was wrong. I felt less than because I wasn't working, wasn't "providing" wasn't paying bills and doing all those things men are supposed to do. I thought that the only things Nicole needed were things she never asked of me. I overlooked her need for peace, support, compassion and care and took all those same things from her selfishly. A relationship thrives on give and take and after moving I realized our relationship wouldn't last through everything we faced if I continued to take more from it than I gave. Men and women have different needs but the one need that will always remain the same among them is the need to be loved. Love is reciprocity. Be sure that in your relationship you're giving back to your partner as much as you've taken.

CHAPTER TEN

Plans Don't Always Work

I sat around for months asking myself one question, "What kind of man would I be if I couldn't stand up to my family on behalf of the woman I loved?" Nicole and I had come so far in two and a half years but no one knew our story. I had hidden her from everyone because I felt like they wouldn't understand our relationship. Now I needed to announce our engagement to my parents. Nicole and I decided we'd travel to Rochester for the Christmas Holiday. We both had to work the day after Christmas, but we had the weekend off and planned on spending it in New York. We booked a hotel room, rented a car, packed our luggage and went off to work on December 26th, 2008.

We left work around 4:30pm headed to Rochester. The day before Nicole and I had gone shopping and purchased small gifts for my parents; we knew we had to put our best foot forward. The conversation that awaited us wasn't going to be an easy one. This would be the first time Nicole met my sister. My sister Lauren is five years older than me and lives in Atlanta and was staying at my parents' house for the Holiday. She was always protective over me like an older sibling tends to be and I loved it when we were younger but as I got ready to introduce my fiancé I knew her being there would present a problem. I explained all of that to Nicole on the drive to New York. Our trip was eventful from the very beginning. Less than twenty miles after we got on the road I was pulled over for speeding in the rain. I remember being panicked because I was going home to see my mother and father for the first time since I moved unexpectedly without telling them. I was certain the trip was doomed from the start. I don't know whether God was smiling over me or if I was being shown just what a good wife can mean for a man but the officer looked my wife-to-be in the eyes and asked her, "Do you know this man, can I trust him?" Nicole answered quickly, "Yes sir, that's my fiancé, he can be trusted, I trust him." The officer looked Nicole in the face and told her, "Tell that man to slow down, he has precious cargo with him and you guys enjoy your weekend."

I saw the wedding ring on the officers' finger and knew what I had just been gifted. That was his wedding present. That was his teaching moment as a man, not as a man of the law but as a man. The punishment I'd endure from putting my woman in a dangerous and compromising position would far exceed anything he could do and he knew that. I knew it too as I drove down the road four hundred miles with Nicole staring at the speedometer. We had a mission to accomplish and couldn't allow foolishness to come between us and our goal. Getting pulled over for speeding in the rain during the heart of the winter in freezing cold weather was foolish. I needed to slow down and my fiancé ensured I knew that. A husband is charged with protecting his wife and that man was letting me know I failed to carry my cargo safely. I understood his point because in so many little ways Nicole proved to me she was the one. I never asked her to prove anything because her actions spoke for themselves. She loved me in all the ways I needed to be loved. Every person requires a special, tailor made kind of love. Nicole filled my gaps.

She took the time to tailor her love specifically for the benefit of our relationship and I had no idea what I'd done to deserve it but I was grateful. Life just had this way of reminding me to take my job seriously. Another lesson learned.

Nicole and I arrived in Rochester around 11pm Friday night. We stopped by to say hello to my parents before heading to the hotel. I introduced her to my sister and we talked for about five minutes before pulling off. They asked us how our ride was; we smiled at each other and said everything went well, no problems. A couple has to know when to keep things private you know? At least Nicole and I had mastered that lesson. It was late and we'd been on the road all day after working so Nicole and I just wanted to pass out. We informed my parents we had a hotel room and were going to get some rest. We said our goodbyes and told them we'd see them tomorrow morning. We were planning on letting everyone know we were engaged on Saturday and wanted to rest before we broke the news. We went off to the hotel, unpacked our bags and got ready for bed. Nicole asked me how I thought my parents would take the news that we were engaged and I told her I honestly didn't know. We were both worried, but there was no turning back now.

The next morning we woke up early, got dressed, left the hotel and headed straight to my parents' house. Nicole and I wanted to announce our engagement in the afternoon, but shortly after we arrived my mother and sister asked Nicole to go to the mall with them. When I asked Nicole if she wanted me to tag along, my mother and sister quickly responded, "What? Do you need to be up under each other all the time?" They wanted their shot at investigating Nicole on their own and I knew if I wanted to announce our engagement, I'd have to allow it. Nicole went off with my mother and sister, and I called two friends to tell them I was in town so we could hang out. I hadn't seen either of them since I moved and wanted to ask them both to be in the wedding. Bread and Daron were two of my closest friends. I left my parents' house and picked my boys up. We drove around for a while, talking, blasting music and deciding where we wanted to go for the night. I called Nicole and told her I was out with my friends for a while. Instantly my boy Daron started judging me. "Aw man you're whipped you have to check in with your woman, that's why I'd never get married." I ignored him and we all went off to the strip club. A dirty, nasty strip club I hated, but Daron bugged me and Bread to take him so that's where we ended up. The Dirty Nail, as if the name doesn't say enough about the place. Not exactly the type of place you want to spend your Christmas weekend you know? We're in the strip club, Daron enjoying himself, while Bread and I drink, bored out of our minds when I got a call. Nicole had been back at my parents' house for an hour and wanted me to come get her. She said she was cool with me hanging out with my friends, but that she just couldn't stand to be around my mother alone any longer and she was tired. I told Bread I had to bounce and get Nicole and he said cool. I went to tell Daron I had to get Nicole and he said," Aw man she got you whipped. Leave me here man."

In that moment I had a decision to choose either my friend or my future wife. I chose my future wife. I got in the car, dropped Bread off at his apartment and went to my parents' house to pick up Nicole. I walked in, and she was in the living room with my mother watching television. I sat down next to Nicole, held her hand, looked my mother in the face and told her that Nicole and I were engaged. It was the first time all day we'd really been alone and I had a chance to share the news. She was tired, but awake. She congratulated Nicole and I and wished us well. Nicole and I both were surprised! We honestly expected a much different reaction but it was very pleasant. I hugged my mom, said goodnight and Nicole and I left to go back to the Dirty Nail to pick up Daron. I told him I'd be back but he didn't believe me. We pulled up to that disgusting strip club and walked in to get my friend. I learned a lot about my wife that night. I learned that she would literally go almost anywhere with me and I appreciated that. I thought about Daron calling me whipped and said to myself, "If you only knew what this woman is about." By the time we drug Daron out of there he was drunk out of his mind, begging me to take him to another club. I agreed just to shut him up as he sat in the car, drunk, telling me that I was whipped with my fiancé in the front seat. Nicole just laughed and told him that I was a grown man and could do whatever I wanted but she just wanted to go to the hotel. I didn't say anything because I knew how Daron was. We finally pulled up to the club he wanted to go to and before I could even park he hopped out of the car and ran off. Nicole looked at me and asked "What's wrong with your friend?" I just told her that's who he is, honestly that's who I used to be too until she came in my life. We laughed about the evening, discussed how surprised we were by my mothers' reaction to the news of our engagement and went off to the hotel for bed.

When Nicole and I woke up on Sunday morning we headed straight to my parents house. When we first got there, my uncle Lonnie was over for breakfast. I remember him taking a look at Nicole and remarking, "Mmmm, that boy done went to Ohio and found him a real woman. Say goodbye to that boy, he's never coming back." My dad laughed and replied, "Yea she is pretty and the girl be dressing." I remember sitting at my parents' dining room table feeling proud. I felt like I had chosen the type of woman worthy of bringing home to family. The type of woman I was supposed to marry. My uncle left and told Nicole and I to stop by his house and say hello to my Aunt Kathy before we hit the road home. We were leaving back to Ohio later in the afternoon after we spent a few hours with my parents', then we were going to stop by my Aunt and Uncle's house to share the good news about our engagement with them. At least that was our plan. Nicole and I were getting ready to leave my parents' house when my sister and mother called us into the living room.

Instantly the conversation turned into all the reasons why they thought Nicole and I shouldn't get married. We weren't old enough, we weren't stable enough financially, we didn't have good enough jobs and we didn't know each other well enough. Nicole and I sat and listened as we were given every reason they thought we shouldn't marry. I remember my mother looking at Nicole and saying, "Well, Richard can be crazy," and Nicole looking my mother in her eyes and responding, "I can be crazy too, Richard knows it." She stood in the face of my family and proclaimed her love in the midst of a blatant attack. I was upset, angry and yelling; Nicole just placed her hand on my shoulder and told me to calm down. I'll never forget when she said, "We don't need this. We told them we were getting married, they can either support us or not, but it's time for us to go." The irony was my sister looked at Nicole and said, "I've never seen someone calm my brother down the way you do, but do you guys have to get married, can't you just live together?" My mother continued to go on about why she thought we were making a mistake. Throughout the entire argument my father was in the kitchen washing dishes. He really didn't have anything to say but he did look at Nicole and tell her, "He's yours now. He doesn't close cabinets, turn off lights, he won't clean up after himself, he doesn't put caps on bottles tightly; just know that's who you're getting." The whole experience was overwhelming but everything I expected it to be. Nicole called to me and just said, "Richard it's time to go home dear."

We got in the car and headed straight back to Ohio. The entire trip we talked about the fallout of what had just taken place. I always told Nicole I doubted my parents would approve, mainly my mother and I was right. I didn't expect my sister to disapprove too, but I wasn't surprised she agreed with mom, she often did. I have gotten use to my sister agreeing with our mother. I left Rochester feeling like I was on my own, like I had no family support for my marriage. I told Nicole that if my mother objected, her side of the family would likely side with her. I had asked two cousins on my fathers' side to be in the wedding but I didn't know how much support we had outside of them. I felt like I was bringing Nicole into a situation she never asked or deserved to be introduced into but the entire time she continued to reassure me that my parents had no impact on the love we shared between the two of us. Our relationship was ours and while their support may have been nice it wasn't required for us to get married. Nicole and I proceeded on with our wedding plans and as the months went by, the drama seemed to continue piling up.

In January of 2009 Nicole lost her job at the call center we'd both been working at. She expected them to fire her because she wasn't the type to be steam-rolled over and she made sure her managers knew that, so she quit before they could. Instantly we went from a two income home to one income. We'd placed a deposit on an apartment and saved a good amount of money to move but Nicole losing her job hurt. We'd also just purchased a new car, which added to our bills. We were still living with her mother and not paying rent so we were able to save but much less than before. And then life continued happening and taking unexpected turns. It was the first week of March when my supervisor made a snide remark to me during a discussion at work that wasn't work related. I should have let the remark go, but I was so unhappy with the job and with my life that I reacted horribly and ended up in a yelling match with my boss in front of the entire office. Besides all of that, this was the same man that disrespected Nicole by calling her a liar one day on the job, so I had issues with him and used the opportunity to make it known. I'll admit as a black man I felt completely disrespect when this white man turned his back on me and walked away as I spoke to him. It angered me and I lashed out. I was asked to leave work promptly and fired the next day for insubordination. Now six months before our wedding both Nicole and I were unemployed again, with no idea on how we were going to finance our big day.

My hot head and lack of self control had placed my family's future in jeopardy once again because I didn't value the true meaning of family. I was still doing what I wanted instead of what my family needed. A man has to learn that in marriage there will be times where what you want has to come second to what your family needs. I hadn't learned that lesson yet and it was hurting Nicole and I. Nicole had been out of work for almost two months and had been looking for a new job and now I was home joining her. It began to feel like every-time we made some progress in our relationship something knocked us backwards. One step forward, two steps back seemed to be our dance routine. Plans don't always work out the way a couple expects and it wasn't taking us long to learn that.

We had all these dreams of how we thought life would go and never took time to prepare for the worst, only thinking that because we believed we were doing everything right things were always going to be right. That's unrealistic and life was educating. I was becoming an antagonist to everyone around me because I felt like I lacked support. Nicole was feeling overwhelmed by working a job she hated and all that comes with that, and I was too. We were arguing more frequently but filed it under "pre-wedding" jitters like many couples likely do. The truth was we weren't suffering from jitters we were suffering from life and all the unexpected things it can throw at you. We were still optimistic and still very much in love but coming to realize that our marriage was not going to be a fairytale. Nicole and I were slowly losing touch with each other emotionally. We were allowing everything around us to affect us so much that our relationship was beginning to suffer. We were being forced by life to learn how to deal with hard times as a couple and the lessons were hard, but necessary. The wedding was six months away and we were looking forward to forever.

***

Recognizing The Root Of The Issue (Nicole)

My reaction on that Sunday was extremely mild. I know many of my ladies are saying "you should have cussed his momma clean the hell out!" Well, the reality of it is that it only appeared she had an issues with me or our pending nuptials. The real issue was for some reason or another her blueprint for her son didn't seem to be holding as much authority over his life as it once did and one could only conclude it was because of me. The fact of the matter was him stepping out into his own light had absolutely nothing to do with me and everything to do with him becoming the man he was no longer afraid to be. That encounter was eye-opening for me. Richard had told me stories of he and his mother's communication tactics and relationship; I just wanted to believe he was exaggerating. I can honestly say I've NEVER heard a mother and son speak to each other the way the two of them had. I felt like I was witnessing a pedestrian filmed video of a street altercation on the internet. In that moment I discovered it wasn't about me and it was never going to be about me. Hell, it was hardly about our relationship, it was about a mother letting go of her son; relinquishing "power." Yes, we've all seen it in movies but since I never experienced it I believed it was make-believe. The relationship between a mother and her baby boy can get a little "sticky" when he is no longer a child. I looked at the hurt, disappointment, and anger in

Richard's eyes and decided then and there that I was going to be his calm in the midst of the storm. I couldn't be selfish and solely concern myself with my feelings, especially when I knew I was equipped to deal with whatever she could possibly dish out. My momma didn't raise a weak woman, so I cower to no one. That was something I could show her better than I could tell her so why waste my time, energy, or intellect?

Don't let other peoples issues become your own and never let those issues infiltrate your union. I know that it may not be easy but it is necessary. I have learned over the years that many of the arguments Richard and I had stemmed from issues that were not our own. No sense in getting all worked up and breaking down communication in your marriage because of someone else's discrepancies. Meanwhile that individual will be going on living their life with little to no concern about you, feeling internally gratified watching you burn in a fire they started. Do not give them the satisfaction. Sit down and have a discussion with your spouse, extinguish the issue immediately. The first thing you should ask is what are we arguing about, and what initiated this argument? If you find that the root cause is not based on something you or your spouse did or said, immediately defuse the situation and avoid the argument.

Happily Ever After? (Richard)

Couples experience trials and tribulations that test their relationship in ways they may have never expected. One of the hardest things for a couple to deal with is what I like to call the "reality check." For a time in every new relationship it seems as if nothing can go wrong. The world appears perfect, happiness comes easy and problems seem like they'll never appear but they always do! Life happens and reality sets in, it is in those moments that a couple's love is put to the test.

Nicole and I had been tested time and time again, and allowed those difficulties to impact us in ways they never should have. We were a young couple who swore we had the world, our love lives, our families and everything around us figured out until time and time again life proved us wrong. In speaking with many young couples over the years I've realized we were not alone in our youthful ignorance. What young couple wants to predict problems they never planned to face before they happen? Then hard times come and you find yourself feeling unprepared. My advice to couples is to be patient, be honest and be encouraged. All couples go through the unexpected. How you deal with the things you could never plan for is when you begin to find out exactly what your union is made of. In a marriage a couple vows to stay together through better or worse, richer or poorer, sickness and health but we never know exactly how those vows will manifest themselves. Even the most thought out plans come unraveled. Whoever wrote the marriage vows must have known that but Nicole and I didn't. We were learning that no matter how careful we were that we couldn't plan everything. Our life together would be filled with unexpected moments and how we dealt with them would define the strength of our relationship. With all that we'd experienced during our engagement the toughest lesson was the one we never planned to learn. Happily ever after doesn't happen effortlessly or without unexpected difficulties.

CHAPTER ELEVEN

Threshold To Forever

Nicole and I continued wedding planning as the months passed. Erica was graduating from college in May, and I knew that would be a great chance for Nicole to meet her and Latoya so they could discuss the wedding. It was really important to me that Nicole had a chance to meet some more of my family so she didn't think we were all crazy. We left Ohio in early May headed to Philadelphia to visit with Erica for her graduation party. When we arrived Erica was out with her friends partying and we stopped at my Uncle Charles and his wife Bethany's house. They were expecting us. I told Nicole when Lawrence's know other Lawrence's are on their way, the front door is always open. We walked straight into my Uncle Charles house true to form, door unlocked for us. We sat around talking all night about the wedding to come. They told us they'd be there, Erica was their daughter. Erica also has a twin brother, Ervin, so if one was in the wedding both were in the wedding and they knew it. Nicole and I didn't want to keep them up all night, so after talking for an hour or two we headed to our hotel. I had looked forward to the trip after our experience in Rochester a few months earlier. It felt good to be around people that supported the relationship Nicole and I shared because they could see I was happy.

The next day I went to pick Latoya up so she could come to the party with Nicole and me. She doesn't drive and when I'm in Philadelphia, I'm her ride. We drove for about twenty minutes and called my cousin to tell her I was lost. She asked me what street I was on. I told her and she replied, "Oh you're right around the corner." I felt like a higher power was hovering over me because as soon as Latoya got in the car she and Nicole hit it off like they'd been friends their entire lives. Nicole was getting along with my cousin, a girl who I considered a sister. I was truly happy. I felt like that Christmas trip in Rochester had been erased for a moment. I remember sitting at my cousins' house that night and Nicole looking at me and saying, "Wow, you and your cousins are so close, you get along like you just saw each other yesterday and haven't seen each other in years." I was so happy when Nicole said that because I looked at her and said, "THIS is our family. I'm the oldest of this crew, we're the example." I didn't know whether or not that was true, but that's how I felt at the time. I felt like maybe Nicole and I were examples for the younger people in our families. That weekend with my cousins was a beautiful one. Nicole was able to meet aunts, uncles and other relatives from the Lawrence family. We ate, drank, shared laughs and most importantly, we felt comfortable as we celebrated Erica's graduation with her.

Before leaving Philadelphia, I looked at Nicole and asked her if she wanted to drive to Brooklyn to visit my grandmother? I wanted to introduce my fiancé to the matriarch, but we didn't have enough money to make the trip. The only person I knew who I could call and ask for the money was my mother, but given the events back in December, I didn't feel comfortable. All I could hear her saying was, "This is why you don't need to get married." That fear prevented me from making a phone call I should have made. A part of me felt like, maybe she was right, maybe I wasn't ready. Feelings of failure began to creep into my mind again, but I put them aside and decided Nicole and I would have another opportunity to see my grandmother so we headed home to Ohio after our blissful weekend. We discussed wedding plans and realized we had more support on my side than we imagined. Finally, our stress was beginning to roll away.

We were headed into June, three months before the wedding when I received a much unexpected phone call. My grandmother had passed away. I felt like crap for allowing the drama between my parents and I to prevent me from attempting everything in my power to see Nana before she passed but I had no one to blame but myself and I knew that. I was determined to put an end to this drama at the funeral by any means necessary. Nicole and I were on the road again headed back to the east coast, this time New Jersey to stay at my uncle's house before the funeral. The funeral was the first time we'd seen my parents since Christmas weekend. Given the sad state of affairs, no one wanted to address what happened back in December. My mother was nice at first; she got Nicole and me a hotel room and gave me some money to get something to eat after our long day of travel. A long day was exactly what we had before traveling to Jersey, because Nicole had emergency dental surgery hours before we left Ohio. I appreciated the gesture of my mom booking us a hotel room; I knew that was her effort to avoid an actual apology or conversation about December's fiasco. I really felt as though maybe things were taking a turn for the better. I never expected Nicole and my mother to have a "happy" relationship, hell, my mother and I didn't have a happy relationship; I simply wanted the two of them to respect each other.

It meant a lot to me that my mother respected the woman I loved, so it truly broke my heart when hours after my grandmothers' funeral was over I walked past my uncle's kitchen and overheard my mom saying, "Did you see her? She's fat isn't she?" On the day my grandmother was buried I had to overhear my mother tell anyone who'd listen how fat my fiancé was. I was hurt and had finally had enough. I called my mother into the back room of my Uncle Junior's house, my father's older brother. I told my mother that I was very heartbroken by what I had overheard and asked her as nicely as I could to respect Nicole or never speak to me again. I told her, "Whether you agree or support my marriage isn't up for me to choose, but I ask if you don't that you don't say anything negative."

That was an emotional conversation, but a much needed one. I had to separate myself from my mother and father and cling to my wife-to-be as the Bible instructs. I never understood that message, but as I was sitting there telling my mother she needed to respect my wife-to-be, it all made sense. My mother agreed and told me she would do her best to give Nicole and our upcoming marriage a chance. That was all I could ask for. I can't say that I was happy, or that I even believed her but I was content. Finally, Nicole and I had jumped our biggest hurdle on the way towards the broom. Three months away from our wedding, we felt like we had nothing to worry about any longer. We still had to figure out the logistics of the wedding, but in comparison to everything we'd been dealing with, that honestly felt like small potatoes.

June left and as July came. Nicole and I moved into our first apartment together. Through our struggles we'd managed to save around $10,000. Just enough to furnish our new apartment and pay rent for two months before the wedding. We placed a deposit on the venue where we wanted to have our reception and went ahead with the planning. A week after we moved into our apartment, my parents stopped in Ohio for a visit. There were uncomfortable moments during the visit, but for the most part things were pleasant. I remember my father walking in the house and saying, "Oh this is nice. Nicole you got nice taste," and my mother replying, "Her taste can't be that nice, she's marrying Richard." I thought nothing of it, just mom being mom. While my parents were there we cooked, invited friends over, and tried to show them that we had built a decent life for ourselves. We discussed wedding plans. My father agreed to get tuxedos for me and my groomsmen since he worked at a tux shop. My mother purchased stamps for us to send off the rest of our wedding invitations. Things finally seemed like they were taking a turn for the better. My parents left Ohio and headed home to New York after a three day visit. Nicole and I finally felt like our marriage was blessed, like our day had no barriers.

Then in August, Nicole's mother called. She said my mother and father had called to speak to her and had said some very unflattering things. My mother talked about how Nicole and I were liars who pretended we were living on our own when we weren't. How Nicole was just using me, which was funny because I had nothing to be used for. A month before Nicole and I were supposed to be wed and we realized that nothing was going to change. Things may get better for a moment, but my mother was never truly going to support our marriage and we had to be alright with that. We had to learn that the opinions of others had no bearing on our love and that was hard, but required. So often couples allow the opinions of others to be the downfall of their relationship and Nicole and I didn't want to be that couple. Those marriage vows we were preparing to say told us to stand together through better or worse and we felt like we were being tested. We could either stand strong or falter. We decided to stand strong, but the drama kept coming. Nicole had found a new job and started graduate school, but I was still unemployed and money for the wedding was running low. The place we planned to have our reception couldn't host us on September 5th, so we had to reschedule the wedding at the last minute to the 19th. Every night it seemed like Nicole and I were arguing. The stress, the exhaustion, her working while

I sat home unemployed, the drama from my parents'; it was a lot to deal with. How we managed to handle it all, I don't know.

I remember our time in pre-marriage counseling with Nicole's pastor. He gave us a survey to fill out, of about 100 questions to be answered separately then brought back and shared with him. We followed his instructions and brought them back to him for review. I'll never forget his response because the first question he asked us was, "Did you two cheat?" Nicole and I looked at each other surprised and quickly responded, "No." Her pastor then told us that in thirty years, he'd never seen a couple who knew as much about each other as she and I did and it'd be his honor to marry us. I remember sitting there with tears in my eyes that day as I explained to Pastor what we'd been going through. I remember him looking at Nicole and asking, "Do you love who this man is today? Because who this man is today is who your husband will be, so do you love this man today?" Nicole said "yes," and then Pastor asked me the same questions. I too said "yes," and it became very clear to me what he meant. Our family situation, our money struggles, or lives weren't going to magically change on September 19th, 2009. The only change in our lives would be that Nicole and I would now be husband and wife, and that was something we had to accept and prepare for. Many couples go into marriage with unrealistic expectations. Life was humbling the hell out of Nicole and I. All those dreams of being young, successful, with high powered careers, seemed to escape us. The dream of having unwavering support from both of our families, seemed like it would never be our reality. However, through it all, the better and the worse, we had each other and for that I was thankful.

Two weeks before the wedding Nicole went to the reception hall to make our final payment. At the last minute the place informed her they needed an additional $1500 to throw the event in addition to what had already been paid. Nicole and I were livid because we didn't have the money and that was not in our original agreement. We felt like we were being strong armed to pay more, but had no other options. We had sent out invitations, set a date and now had no reception hall. Without knowing where to turn, I called my father's brother, Uncle Junior. I explained the situation to him and told him I needed his help. I was embarrassed to even make the call because I had never asked him for anywhere near that sort of money before. He told me he had some work that needed to be done around his house and he wasn't sure if he could get the money to me, but that he would call my parents and talk to them. I thanked my uncle, without knowing what the result would be. True to his word he called my parents and talked to them for me. I don't know what the conversation consisted of, but I do know a few days before the wedding a check for $1500 showed up to my apartment from my mother. I remember looking at Nicole and asking her, "Do you think we should cash this? I mean with all that's been said and done?" Nicole looked at me and said, "WE deserve this, consider it compensation for emotional distress. Let's re-plan our wedding."

That week before the wedding was special. Nicole and I pulled off something mildly miraculous. We purchased food, rented tables and chairs, got decorations and turned her church basement into the most beautiful reception hall we could manage. I catered the wedding to the best of my ability, and several of Nicole's friends and family made food donations. It wasn't the wedding we planned, but it was the wedding we made possible, and it was beautiful. If there's one thing our engagement taught us, it's that things don't always go as planned in life and love. A couple that lasts has to adapt. Nicole and I had proven we could adapt and I was proud of us. I remember receiving phone calls from family and friends letting us know that we had their support. By then everyone knew I was at odds with my parents and just wanted to check on Nicole and I to make sure we were alright. I kept telling myself I lacked support but time would show nothing was further from the truth. Through our drama and eventful engagement the doubt that filled our relationship began to subside. I felt like if Nicole and I could make it over that broom, we could make it through any and everything. It was 9.18.2009.

My parents arrived in town the day before and texted to let me know they were there, but we didn't speak. The remainder of the Lawrence family showed up in Ohio on the 18th. My mother is the youngest of seven, but only one member from her family sent a representative. That was hurtful to me but I can honestly say it was completely expected and probably best. The last thing I needed on the weekend of my marriage was more drama. My sister also didn't show. Back in August when my mother contacted Nicole's mom, my sister and I got into a heated argument. Nicole and my sister had exchanged heated words on Facebook and my sister was very disrespectful to my fiancé, so in turn I was very disrespectful to her. I was getting married and my only sister wasn't going to be there to see it. That hurt but when I looked around and saw all the family who did come to Ohio to support me I truly felt a sense of peace.

I invited my family to the wedding rehearsal, and the rehearsal dinner that followed. I remember my mother walking into the church late, loudly announcing, "Your family is here," which was ironic to me because almost none of her family showed up. My father's family was there to support me, but I never doubted they would be. That night was eventful. I remember Nicole telling me that my Aunt Bethany had seen her in the bathroom flustered due to the remarks my mother continuously made under her breath. My Aunt just let her know if she needed anything, she was there for her, and to not stress over the drama. Nicole pulled herself together, we finished eating dinner and I prepared for the bachelor party with my groomsmen. Nicole got her bridesmaids' together and they left to spend the night getting ready for our big day.

The bachelor party was supposed to be a night of fun, at least that's what I planned but once again if you want to make God laugh tell him what you have planned. My groomsmen and several friends prepared to go to a club, but spent all night arguing over which one. Daron wanted to see strippers and refused to go anywhere else so finally we all relented and ended up at a strip club. From the moment Daron arrived he had an attitude. Looking back, I truly think he was disappointed he wasn't my best man. Honestly, I didn't make him best man because I didn't think he was right for the job. From the moment he arrived in Ohio he carried on like he was on a vacation and not as a wedding party participant. We ended up doing what he wanted during the bachelor party, not what I wanted and I was the groom. As we left the club, I let Daron have it out of frustration. I told him how selfish and how disrespectful he had been since he arrived in Ohio. He threatened me to a fight, but the rest of my groomsmen wouldn't allow it. I was hours away from marrying the woman I loved, I could not risk jail. Daron and I continued arguing because he was upset over what I had said to him. I told him that he was selfish, and was disrespecting my marriage. Told him I couldn't understand why he didn't value family when he came from such a strong one himself. That struck a nerve. Around 3am that morning he got in his car and drove away headed back to New York, leaving my cousin Tim and my Best-Man Bread behind because they had rode to Ohio with him. I had lost a groomsman less than twelve hours before my wedding, as if Nicole and I needed any more obstacles. I refused to let Daron put a damper on our day. I went to bed around 4am on the 19th, setting my alarm to rise at 10am to prepare for the wedding. When my alarm went off the next morning I called Nicole's maid of honor Ellen and told her we were down one groomsman. I explained to her what went on the night before and then told her, "Do not tell

Nicole, just make it work, please!" When we showed up to the church around noon, the first person we saw was my mother. She asked where Daron was and none of the groomsmen answered. She continued to ask, and finally my cousin Ervin stepped in and said, "Auntie, let it go, everyone who needs to be here is here."

Those words rang so true. I thought about all the friends and family who weren't in First AME Zion Church on that day and a sense of peace dawned over me. I thought about everything I'd gone through with my family, with friends; thought about the years Nicole and I had spent in a long distance relationship and realized that no one ever really expected us to share a wedding day. Not even we expected to share a wedding day. To everyone else in the world the day may have been a celebration but to us it was an accomplishment. Almost four years before that day Nicole and I set out on a friendship that turned into a courtship that evolved into love. We were in love and soon to be wed. As I walked to the altar and the ceremony began, I felt overjoyed. As soon as I saw Nicole coming down the aisle, I grabbed my handkerchief and began to wipe the tears from my eyes. Our life may not have been picture perfect but it was reality.

Nicole stepped to the altar and we exchanged vows and rings. Nicole asked me to write my vows and for once, nothing came to my mind. I remember taking the microphone and simply telling her what I felt at the time. "I love you. You're my best-friend. You mean the world to me. We've been through so much but you've never left my side and for that I'm grateful. I vow to spend my life trying to make you the happiest woman in this world. I LOVE YOU!" Nicole sang "Inseparable," by Natalie Cole. I cried tears of joy. Nicole broke out during the song crying and started to go off-note which is why she told me she never wanted to sing at her own wedding, but she did it because I asked. I just remember thinking to myself, "She's amazing. She can "mess up" in a room full of people, regain composure and walk out with her head held high. That's MY wife!" After we finished reciting our vows the Pastor went on with the ceremony. As the wedding drew to a close the Pastor looked into the congregation and recited loudly over Nicole and I, "What God has brought together, LET NO MAN, LET NO MAN, I REPEAT, LET NO MAN PUT ASUNDER." And with that, Nicole and I were now husband and wife. To have and to hold, in sickness and health, for richer or poorer, till death do us part.

We'd dreamed of that day, but what the future held, we had no idea. The reception was fun, a wonderful party filled with friends and family. We even invited guests to our home that evening and continued partying until around 3am. Nicole and I were so tired; we didn't even have the energy to make love and that was ALRIGHT with us. We had a lifetime to enjoy that in our marriage.

We woke up late the next afternoon on the 20th and went out to dinner at one of our favorite restaurants. As we were eating, we had a picture taken. A little girl at the table next to us asked her mother, "Why are they taking pictures?" I could hear the girls' mother say to her, "I think they just got married." It seemed like the perfect ending of an eventful but magical weekend. Nicole and I returned home to finally consummate or new union. That night, making love to my wife. I truly felt like I had grown up. I didn't have the perfect job, car, house or anything, but I had the woman I loved and we were perfectly happy, we'd made it from cyber to ceremony...matrimony was our new chapter in life!

ABOUT THE AUTHORS

Richard and Nicole Lawrence are the founder and CEO of Forever Young, Black & Married LLC. in Columbus, Ohio. Both graduates of historically black universities, the two are a young dynamic duo devoted to spreading the message of love and matrimony especially in the African-American community. Upon establishing a strong social media presence the twosome began to receive request to be guest speakers on radio broadcast and featured writers in respected marriage/relationship publications. Undeniably sharing a love for writing and each other the couple decided it was time to share their journey to the altar via the pages of a memoir. In their first publication they utilize the transparency of their relationship to share their love story as well as useful tips, to assist couples along their journey through love.

www.foreveryoungblackandmarried.com

ACKNOWLEDGEMENTS

(The author's collective acknowledgements)
We would like to thank every single YB&M family member! Your support has been a true blessing to the two of us.

Special thanks to Diana Perez, Tiffany Henry, Chris Hairston and Tonya L. Etter! Your testimonials were amazing and truly humbling. So great that we had to feature them on the back cover.

(Richard's acknowledgements)
First I'd like to thank God for loving me even when I didn't love myself and for guiding me when I was lost.

To my wife Nicole: This journey has been long, stressful, full of nagging and arguments and stress from us both and yet like always you've found the strength to stand by me. I love you in ways words could never begin to express, but I'm wordy so forgive me if I spend the rest of my life trying to capture the essence of the greatest gift I could ever have been blessed with, YOU. I love YOU. Thank YOU!

To my family and friends: I won't even begin to name people because I'd leave someone out and for that blame my mind and not my heart. Thank you for the love and support. You've seen me through the worst over the years, and for that I am forever grateful.

Thank you ALL. to the Young, black and married family: When I started blogging in 2010 I never imagined the day I'd be sharing thoughts with so many. You all have become a blessing to my marriage. I thought years ago that maybe through blogging I'd be able to help others find happiness in their relationships but you all have taught me to appreciate my own and for that I am thankful from the bottom of my heart. People often ask me, "Why did you name it Young, black and married?" As a young, black married man I felt alone. I read the blogs and social media posts and it seemed like nobody was speaking for me. People kept telling me I was 'special' and I just didn't believe that. I knew I wasn't alone, I knew there were other couples out there like Nicole and I and I wanted to reach out to them. Never did I imagine so many would reach back and to each and EVERY one of you, thank you!

(Nicole's acknowledgements)
First, giving all honor and glory to my savior. God, you see in me what I couldn't see in myself. You continue to bless my life and spirit. Through it all and I. am blessed. I can testify that you've been good!

To my King, my best friend, my help-mate, my husband. You are my muse, my reason, my good thing. I love you to life and I will be here, no questions. You have been my biggest cheerleader and an amazing support system. I never thought I could love so completely but God has the final say. You make me feel like the smartest, prettiest girl in the world and I will live out our days returning the love. What is understood doesn't need explaining. I'm IN LOVE with you Boobie and I like you too!

To my Shero, my mommy, Mrs. Mary I.! You're an amazing human being and God broke the mold when he created you. You have taught me how to love, encouraged me to live and supported me through it all. You epitomize motherhood. You gave me the blueprint on how to be a wife via your actions in loving my daddy. Thank you for the stable home life!

To my daddy Mr. Wesley Al. You may have perished from Earth but you forever dwell in my heart. I love you because of the father you were to my brother and I and the husband you were to my mother. God knew what he was doing when he entrusted my up-bringing in your hands. Forever missing you, Nic Nic.

To my ENTIRE family. you're such a blessing to me. I have no words to describe what having you in my life and corner means. Just know I love you and I am a blessed woman.

To my A-1's since day one. Brittney, Candis and Monique no truer friends exist. We have been through playground drama and college parties together and still going strong. God blessed me with the brightest of light when he brought you ladies into my life, I love you each 4-life, Bookie!

www.ingramcontent.com/pod-product-compliance
Lightning Source LLC
Chambersburg PA
CBHW031624040426
42452CB00007B/666